Nothing is outside of God's jurisdiction. There's nothing He doesn't see, know, or have His hand in. Even the hard things. It's all within His reach.

Think of an orchestra conductor. She knows the music from front to back. She knows the cues to bring in certain instruments. Her body mimics the tone and intensity of each passage. The entire orchestra watches every flick of her finger or expression on her face. Each musician looks to her to set the rhythm of the entire beautiful story.

Our God is like that. He's a Master Conductor with every moment planned out in the symphony of history. Your life fits perfectly into the rhythm of His plans and the work of His hands.

*The counsel of the Lord stands forever,
the plans of His heart from
generation to generation.*

PSALM 33:11

Have you ever been asked to do something you just knew you didn't have the skills for? Did you feel defeated before you began, or challenged to try something new?

Sometimes the commands we read in the Bible can feel impossible. Try using your own strength to not worry when that diagnosis comes in; when that job is on the line; when that relationship takes a turn for the worse.

But what God asks, He can always deliver. When He says, "Do not be anxious," we can be confident that He's got a way for joy and thanksgiving to replace feelings of fear and worry. It's up to us to ask for and receive His grace for the moment.

Be anxious for nothing,
but in everything by prayer and supplication
with thanksgiving let your requests be made
known to God. And the peace of God,
which surpasses all comprehension, will guard
your hearts and your minds in Christ Jesus.

PHILIPPIANS 4:6-7

God is a gentleman. He's not a God who manipulates, fights, punishes, or argues in order to gain the upper hand in a relationship. He is the perfect example of love and servant-hearted leadership.

That said, God will often let us run out of the options at our own fingertips if we're determined to figure things out without Him. It's like a carpenter's level. If we are heavy-handed in our control of a situation, it limits God's willingness to pour on His power. But when we balance our willingness with His strength, there's no limit to what we can do together.

He has said to me,
"My grace is sufficient for you,
for power is perfected in weakness."
Most gladly, therefore,
I will rather boast about my weaknesses,
so that the power of Christ may dwell in me.
II CORINTHIANS 12:9

Nothing happens apart from God's knowledge. Take a minute to think about what it would be like to have a God who could be surprised by circumstances. "What?" He might say. "Wait, I didn't know (insert your name here) was going through such a thing. Who let that happen? Why wasn't I informed? Oh dear, what am I going to do now??"

Hopefully that sounds ridiculous to you! Because even though hard or painful things happen, Romans 8:28 promises that God can work every single detail of your life into good, good things. It takes trust. It takes leaning in sometimes, asking tough questions, and believing extravagantly.

Who is there who speaks and it comes to pass, unless the Lord has commanded it?

LAMENTATIONS 3:37

Cake! Balloons! Streamers! Singing! Presents! Special activities! There are so many ways birthdays are celebrated. The goal on someone's birthday is to help them feel extra loved, known, and appreciated. Another word for that might be favored.

With God, those who have a relationship with Him are favored 24/7/365. It's like having the very best dad with the very best treasure trove of everything you could ever need or want. Often His gifts are spiritual, unseen, feelings of peace or grace. Other times He steps into situations and makes His favor for you known in tangible ways. But no matter what, you can go about today knowing that if you love the Lord, you are favored in His eyes.

The Lord favors those who fear Him,
those who wait for His lovingkindness.

PSALM 147:11

*L*ife is about a personal relationship with Jesus. But He built in a great plan where we need to spend time with other people who love Him. Being authentic, sharing our imperfect moments, and praying together are some of the best ways to strengthen our relationships and build trust with one another.

It's been said, "No man is an island." We're a lot more like a continent made up of all sorts. Together we are colorful, bright, rich, and strong. We need each other!

Therefore, confess your sins to one another, and pray for one another so that you may be healed. The effective prayer of a righteous man can accomplish much.

JAMES 5:16

If you're like most people, you've experienced a time (or times) in your life when knowing Jesus was not a priority. Many people describe their "before" life as dark and full of emptiness—and their new life in Christ as light and free.

Genesis 1:1 describes a time when the earth was "formless and void." Then the Spirit hovered, God spoke, and life happened!

As we grow deeper with Jesus, we experience the life-creating love that sets us free. It's a process. It can be messy at times. But with Jesus, we are always becoming more and more like Him. It gets easier to prioritize His heart, His kingdom, and His purpose above our own.

I count all things to be loss in view of the surpassing value of knowing Christ Jesus my Lord, for whom I have suffered the loss of all things, and count them but rubbish so that I may gain Christ.

PHILIPPIANS 3:8

The crowds are pressing. The stadium is loud. But as you are ushered behind a curtain and through a door, you begin to notice sounds of stage hands moving equipment and behind-the-scenes organizers setting things in order. You are led down a hallway to a door with a star on it. You know that as soon as the knob turns, you'll be face to face with the hero you've always wanted to meet.

With God, we always have VIP access. All the way in. Anytime, anyplace, for any reason. No special badges or ID: if you know Jesus, you've got all the permission you need.

Therefore let us draw near with confidence to the throne of grace, so that we may receive mercy and find grace to help in time of need.

HEBREWS 4:16

It's most likely that if you are in need of groceries, you get in the car and head to the nearest Walmart, Aldi, or Safeway. If you want to see a movie, you either turn on Netflix or look up a new release at the local theater.

It makes good sense that when we need hope, we go to the source of all hope. Hope is God's specialty. He invented it. When things looked bleak, Jesus came along bearing all the possibility of freedom and eternal life. And it didn't end at the cross. Hope is a necessary part of life. It fills and sustains us. And we're meant to share it with the world around us. So go to the source today, and get you some hope!

Now may the God of hope fill you
with all joy and peace in believing,
so that you will abound in hope
by the power of the Holy Spirit.
ROMANS 15:13

*Y*ou haven't heard a peep from behind the closed door for an hour now. Quietly you place your hand on the knob. You lean your shoulder against the door, pressing gently to help it open without creaking. Moonlight hits the wall through cracked curtains. As you enter this peaceful world, you can hear whisper-soft breathing and detect the kick of a tiny, swaddled foot from inside the crib. You peer over the edge...and just watch. You could stay here forever...full of more love than you ever thought possible.

This is how your Father sees you too. With more love than you could ever imagine and more tenderness than your heart could ever hold.

> He will not allow your foot to slip;
> He who keeps you will not slumber...
> The Lord will guard your going out and your
> coming in from this time forth and forever.

PSALM 121:3, 8

A certain battery brand used to advertise that its batteries would keep going way beyond the average battery life. The brand was made famous by its pink bunny mascot, wearing sunglasses and playing a drum, tirelessly wandering across the television screen. Viewers were meant to believe that this battery would go on practically forever.

Of course, we know that batteries eventually give up. The only unending source of power and strength comes from God! He's the very best One to turn to if we need to keep going. His power has a built-in recharge. All we need to do is stay plugged in and connected to Him. God will sustain us.

Do you not know? Have you not heard? The Everlasting God, the Lord, the Creator of the ends of the earth does not become weary or tired. His understanding is inscrutable.

ISAIAH 40:28

Every business has a president. Every country has a leader. Every school has a principal. Each of these decision-makers is important to its organization.

But in the end, there is always someone with more authority. A business owner is subject to state laws. A principal is subject to the school board. And a country's leader, regardless of their belief or understanding, is under the power of the Lord.

Psalm 2:4 says that "He who sits in the heavens laughs, the Lord scoffs at" leaders who think they are in control.

No matter how circumstances may seem, good or bad—our God has the reins, because He reigns!

Who has announced this from of old?
Who has long since declared it?
Is it not I, the Lord? And there is no other
God besides Me, A righteous God and
a Savior; There is none except Me.

ISAIAH 45:21

"Ugh, not again!" How many times have you done that thing...said what you shouldn't have, reacted to poor driving in a less-than-Christian way...it happens to the best of us!

You've probably heard it said that God loves us right where we are, but loves us too much to leave us there. The beauty of knowing Jesus is that we are definitely works in progress. That's a promise! By the power of the Holy Spirit we are being changed. We're growing and maturing. And it's often the harder things in life that shape our change process.

So take heart. You're not alone. And as long as you aim to love God well, He will continue to do a good work in you.

For those whom He foreknew,
He also predestined to become conformed
to the image of His Son, so that He would be
the firstborn among many brethren.

ROMANS 8:29

Two sisters were taken to Disneyland by their parents. The older girl worried about the rides. Would she get sick? She worried about being away from home. Would the dog miss them too much? Would the airplane ride be scary?

The younger girl imagined it would be wonderful. She thought of the characters, balloons, treats and fun rides. She thought of the stories she'd have to tell when she got back. Mostly she thought about the unknown possibilities.

Who do you think had more fun?

Worry is a life-stealer, a fun-thief. God suggests we not worry, because there's no good that comes from it. All the good comes from living expectantly for our amazing God to be His amazing self.

Who of you by being worried can add a single hour to his life?

MATTHEW 6:27

Imagine getting behind the wheel of a fast car, and then adamantly refusing to hold onto the steering wheel. Chaos would ensue! Most likely you'd end up in a ditch or knocking over someone's mailbox.

Trust, on the other hand, requires no steering wheel. It's like stepping onto a roller coaster and raising those hands way into the air. You can be sure you're safe and buckled into God's love. You can anticipate the dips and speed without worrying about the outcome. You are free to enjoy the journey with laughter and loved ones.

Try letting go on purpose today, and see what adventures unfold.

Commit your way to the Lord, trust also in Him, and He will do it. He will bring forth your righteousness as the light and your judgment as the noonday.

PSALM 37:5-6

In this demanding and distracting world, rest is so important. But many people aren't sure how to rest in a way that fills and refreshes them.

Resting in Jesus isn't too unlike resting on a beach, in a hammock, with a cool glass of water and a good book in hand. Your mind releases its worries—to Jesus. Your body relaxes, as if wrapped in strong arms. Your thoughts turn to all the good qualities of the One who loves you more than anything.

Resting in Jesus can happen at the office or at home, in nature or on a busy street. Try taking 5 minutes today and deliberately practicing the art of resting in Jesus.

Come to Me, all who are weary and heavy-laden, and I will give you rest.

MATTHEW 11:28

God's values tend to be quite a bit different from our own. Consider the widow who could afford to put one single coin into the offering box. Jesus called her the most generous woman on earth! Her heart was wealthy, even if her pocketbook was empty.

God's idea of success isn't always the top rung of the corporate ladder or the best voice in the talent show. He looks at us from the inside out, and loves seeing our motivations in line with His own.

Before you begin your next venture, decide up front with the Lord what success will look like. It may not be money or fame; instead, it may be having fun, loving well, or giving it your very best.

Do not store up for yourselves treasures on
earth, where moth and rust destroy,
and where thieves break in and steal.
But store up for yourselves treasures in heaven,
where neither moth nor rust destroys,
and where thieves do not break in or steal.

MATTHEW 6:19-20

You're contagious! Did you know? But in the very best way.

Every time you encourage someone. Every time you let someone cut in line in front of you. Every time you make a decision based on whatever is true, right, noble, lovely, pure, excellent, or praiseworthy (Phil. 4:8)...the goodness of God is poured out.

Of course, it works the other way too. Negative words and actions can have an effect on those around us. It can be a challenge to live out the love of Jesus when circumstances are testing our emotions and patience. But every time we choose love, everyone wins.

In speech, conduct, love, faith and purity, show yourself an example of those who believe.

I TIMOTHY 4:12

The hiker stops in the middle of a snowy meadow. She looks left and right. But with fresh snow blanketing the path, she's not sure which way is forward. And of course she's too far away for cellular service to activate the GPS map on her phone.

Thankfully, this hiker came prepared. She knows how to read a compass. So she pulls it out, checks the needle, and turns slightly east. "This is the way," she says to herself, newly confident.

Emotions, circumstances, and—of course—people, can cause us to wonder what to do next. But like a girl and her compass, we can turn to the Word for next steps. There's never a time when kindness, love, and forgiveness are a bad path to take.

As those who have been chosen of God, holy and beloved, put on a heart of compassion, kindness, humility, gentleness and patience; bearing with one another, and forgiving each other, whoever has a complaint against anyone; just as the Lord forgave you, so also should you.

COLOSSIANS 3:12-13

Imagine your life being recorded on a white board in permanent marker. You told a fib...that goes on the board. You cut someone off in traffic...oops, that's strike two for today! And never mind the "big" sins. In permanent ink. Recorded forever in your book of life!

Have you ever accidentally written on a dry erase board with permanent ink? Here's a tip: nail polish remover. Wipe a little on the board, and even the toughest scribble disappears.

That, friend, is how God sees forgiveness. Once forgiven, your past trouble disappears. No matter how bad it felt to you. No sin can remain under the blood of Jesus.

I will forgive their iniquity,
and their sin I will remember no more.

JEREMIAH 31:34

You've probably heard it said that the only thing you can count on is change. That may be true by the world's standards. But we know that God never changes. His character is as true and sure as it was before the earth was created. Every word He says can be counted on. Everything He has promised will be delivered.

God is often referred to in the Psalms as a rock or a fortress. He can be trusted, leaned on, and run to. If there's anything unsure in your life, you can know that it's not God who is shifting.

Jesus Christ is the same yesterday
and today and forever.
HEBREWS 13:8

Sometime, if you haven't before, try looking up videos of children being told they're being adopted. Oh, and have a box of tissues handy. Because it's one of the most beautiful things you may ever see. No one can understand like the fatherless, quite what it's like to be welcomed into family.

No matter your past or upbringing, God is a good, good Father who loves and accepts each of His children with open arms. No abuse or manipulation are part of His parenting. All of His discipline happens out of love.

In the family of God, you can count on a kind of love you've never known before.

You have not received a spirit of slavery leading to fear again, but you have received a spirit of adoption as sons by which we cry out, "Abba! Father!"

ROMANS 8:15

God is full of wise advice. He's not in the business of puffing Himself up for His own sake, but He knows and wants what is the very best for us.

That's why, when He says praise and thanks are good medicine you can believe it. Maybe you've experienced it before. You're having a terrible day. And in a moment of clarity you decide to focus on the good things. You think of things to be thankful for. You turn your thanks toward God. Pretty soon, the more you focus on His goodness, the better you feel.

The Bible actually tells us to dance, sing, and praise Him! There are times to be quiet and stoic. There are also times to lavish God with extravagant praise.

Let them praise His name with dancing;
Let them sing praises to Him with timbrel
and lyre. For the Lord takes pleasure in His
people; He will beautify the afflicted ones with
salvation. Let the godly ones exult in glory;
Let them sing for joy on their beds.

PSALM 149:3-5

Preventive medicine can save a person a lot of heartache (or headache, or any other body ache)! Letting a doctor check for trouble can keep you much healthier in the long run.

Spending time with God through prayer, listening, reading the Word, and many other ways can get you ready for anything that comes along. Taking Him seriously builds your trust in what He says and who He is. It's kind of like adding tools to your tool chest, just in case. You never know what life will bring, and being as ready as possible by knowing Him as well as you can, will bring a whole lot of peace when you get there.

I will meditate on Your precepts and regard
Your ways. I shall delight in Your statutes;
I shall not forget Your word.
PSALM 119:15-16

Have you ever known of a child who falls into the wrong crowd of friends? You may have observed behavior and attitude changes to the point that you hardly recognize the sweet one you once knew. Likewise, a great group of friends can challenge a child to grow and encourage her to be her best.

The company you keep makes a difference too. Being around Jesus brings out the best in anyone. He's the very best example, and leads you along the very best path.

*Keep watching and praying
that you may not enter into temptation;
the spirit is willing,
but the flesh is weak.*

MATTHEW 26:41

Do you ever tell yourself what to do? In the Psalms, David did it all the time. He knew that sometimes his own soul needed encouraging. Yes, that may have been a product of living and working in remote pastures by himself! But the point is, David understood the benefit of declaring the truth.

It's not always easy or natural to focus on the positive. Circumstances can be overwhelming. Relationships can be emotional. But God is always good, and always works things for good. And praising Him in the midst of any storm can work wonders for your soul and attitude.

The next time you find yourself struggling, try talking to yourself. Build yourself up, and remind your soul who's Boss (God, of course)!

Bless the Lord, O my soul, And all that is within me, bless His holy name. Bless the Lord, O my soul, and forget none of His benefits.

PSALM 103:1-2

There's something special about an underdog. You know, that team that hasn't won any games this season but has an amazing attitude and works so hard. Or the child in class who never gets picked first. Or the cancer patient whose dream is fulfilled by a loving community. Heartstrings get tugged when good people get lifted up.

This tendency may very well be God-wired in us. After all, Jesus came for the broken, the lonely, the hurting, and the lost. He is drawn to the ones with sincere hearts. He loves to love those in need. And He's made us to follow in His footsteps.

*Though the Lord is exalted,
yet He regards the lowly,
but the haughty He knows from afar.*

PSALM 138:6

We've all been there. On the playground or in the ballpark, waiting for the team captains to take turns choosing kids for their teams. Maybe you were a first pick. Maybe you were the fastest or the most skilled. If you were like most of us, you fit somewhere in the middle of the pack...or even toward the end.

On God's team, no one is ranked by ability. Everyone is simply chosen. First. Every time. You've got the precise skillset you were designed to have, and your team needs you just as you are!

Life has a lot of practices and many games. Get to know your teammates, and enjoy the process!

*For you are a holy people
to the Lord your God; the Lord your God
has chosen you to be a people for His own
possession out of all the peoples who are
on the face of the earth.*

DEUTERONOMY 7:6

In a race, there can be only one first place winner. But in the kingdom, winning is about finishing well. What does that mean? Perhaps it means devoting life to loving the Lord our God with all our heart, soul, mind and strength. And loving others as ourselves. Maybe it means serving others with a heart like Jesus.

Regardless, you can be sure that the prize is within your reach. So stay strong, press on, and keep believing. You've got what it takes to be a kingdom-class athlete. Train hard and follow Coach Holy Spirit's instructions. You may just have a medal coming!

I press on toward the goal
for the prize of the upward call
of God in Christ Jesus.
PHILIPPIANS 3:14

Some teachers are known for their soft hearts and easy A's. Other teachers have reputations that make incoming students dread their next semester.

The thing is, "soft" and "tough" don't necessarily equate to "good" and "bad." God is both a tender-hearted Father and an uncompromising judge. Take a look at the story of the servants who were given money to care for in their Master's absence (Matt. 25:14-30). The servants who acted wisely received a great reward. The servant who acted foolishly lost what he was given in the first place.

There's a peace that comes in knowing where the boundaries are, and God sets perfect boundaries. His rules are in place so that we can be free and happy in His kingdom.

Therefore we also have as our ambition, whether at home or absent, to be pleasing to Him. For we must all appear before the judgment seat of Christ, so that each one may be recompensed for his deeds in the body, according to what he has done, whether good or bad.

II CORINTHIANS 5:9-10

Gold mining involves a whole lot of work to remove the valuable pieces from the rubble. Heavy water pressure is applied, as well as sifting, stirring, and much more. But in the end, any tiny flakes of gold are treated like the treasures they are. Many of us wear gold as a symbol of marriage commitment, or as a special adornment.

We ourselves are gold to our God. He works tirelessly to refine us. His hands get dirty in the mud, sifting out the junk and searching for the valuable pieces He can use. And in the end, we are His most treasured possession.

But He knows the way I take;
When He has tried me, I shall come forth
as gold. My foot has held fast to His path;
I have kept His way and not turned aside.

JOB 23:10-11

Tuck yourself into the arms of the Father, and you'll never be alone. Not in the worst of times. Not when the job ends and the bills are due. Not when he comes home late—again. Or when she still can't seem to stop drinking.

You'll be cared for richly. Your roots will go down deep into His love and stay there. And as you learn, you'll grow. God will take care of every one of your needs. Not only will you survive the drought, but you will truly thrive. You'll become an example for the world, a light, a bright spot that people look to. And that's when you can point to Jesus.

And the LORD will continually guide you, and satisfy your desire in scorched places, and give strength to your bones; and you will be like a watered garden, and like a spring of water whose waters do not fail.

ISAIAH 58:11

Have you ever found yourself pressed beyond your limits? Marathoners experience that at the beginning of a training season. They might wonder, after their first 3-mile run, how they will ever go 26.2 miles without stopping. But eventually, they do!

Those who grieve the loss of a loved one know about limits. There are times when "enough is enough" crosses the mind. But they still keep going through the process of pain and healing.

Grace is a miraculous thing. God provides grace for the moment, right when we need it—rarely too early, and never too late. And it always lasts as long as we need.

The experience of spiritual stamina isn't always easy or fun. But to know His grace in the process can be very rewarding.

Those who wait for the LORD will gain new strength; they will mount up with wings like eagles, they will run and not get tired, they will walk and not become weary.

ISAIAH 40:31

There are obvious choices. Will it be healthier to eat this avocado toast or this sprinkle donut? And there are much more subtle choices. Ones that sneak up on us unaware. Like the thoughts going through our minds.

We can't always control the thoughts that come into our minds, but we can decide what to do about them. We can choose to take captive the thoughts that beat us down, and replace them with thoughts that build us up. Next time you find yourself thinking glass-half-empty things, try turning that glass upside down.

Whatever is true, whatever is honorable, whatever is right, whatever is pure, whatever is lovely, whatever is of good repute, if there is any excellence and if anything worthy of praise, dwell on these things.

PHILIPPIANS 4:8

Some people walk into a room, and immediately the atmosphere is different. Maybe it's their smile or laughter. Maybe it's their gregarious, outgoing personality. Or maybe it's a grouchy, grumpy, never-satisfied party pooper.

This is a very simple way to say that we can either influence those around us or be influenced. We can melt into the crowd or stand out from it. We can live quiet Christian lives, calling our faith "private" or "personal"—which it most definitely is! But we can also be unashamed and open about living our faith for the world to see.

As ambassadors for Christ, we get to represent Him here and now.

Beloved, while I was making every effort to write you about our common salvation, I felt the necessity to write to you appealing that you contend earnestly for the faith which was once for all handed down to the saints.

JUDE 1:3

If you've ever cheated on a test (no, of course not, right??) you know that the reward isn't quite as sweet as working hard and doing your very best.

Life isn't meant to be cheated, although there are lots of ways to cut corners out there! No text message could ever compete with showing up at a memorial service and giving your friend a hug of sympathy and sorrow.

The easy way isn't always the best way, and the best way isn't always hard. The trick is to stay focused on Jesus and walk where He walks. If you do, you'll definitely benefit from the reward of walking well.

Suffer hardship with me, as a good soldier of Christ Jesus...if anyone competes as an athlete, he does not win the prize unless he competes according to the rules. The hard-working farmer ought to be the first to receive his share of the crops.

II TIMOTHY 2:3, 5-6

In a crazy uncertain world, there's one place with all the answers. Or more correctly, one Person.

God never lies. He never misses. He never predicts a thing and finds Himself having to back-pedal or explain Himself. God is no half-accurate weatherman!

Every word He speaks is true. Every word of His Word is true. And He promises that if we ask we'll receive; if we seek we'll find; if we knock the door will be opened.

God doesn't always respond in the ways we expect or want. But anything we get from Him is right on the money.

> I, the LORD, speak righteousness,
> declaring things that are upright.
>
> ISAIAH 45:19

The conductor raises his baton, and the first notes of a violin float over the audience. As the music swells, the atmosphere charges. Drums beat. Trumpets ring out. Clarinets and coronets and keyboards chime in. Some are brought to tears by the end of the performance.

Music reaches the heart in a way that any other input does not. Maybe this is why the Bible reflects the power of music to praise and worship God, strengthen our own spirits, and celebrate or mourn with others.

Whatever the reason, music can bring us closer to the Creator. Whether you can carry a tune or not, your heart is always carried to the One who created you to worship Him.

I will sing of lovingkindness and justice, to You, O LORD, I will sing praises.

PSALM 101:1

There's nothing quite like the power of prayer. It's a direct conversation with the greatest source of strength we could ever hope for. Apart from His strength, there's very little we could accomplish on our own. We would be powerless against temptation, at least on a long-term basis. We'd be tossed around by any influence we came across.

But with God all things are possible. With God, we can lean in for all sorts of amazing and miraculous things. When He says we can avoid temptation it's because He's put a failsafe in the plan—pray to, trust in, and lean on Him.

Pray that you may not
enter into temptation.

LUKE 22:40

In a nutshell, God is HUGE. Just think! He holds the universe in the palm of His hand! Can you imagine the volume of love that is contained in such a vast being?

If you've had children, you've probably experienced the phenomenon of feeling more love than you ever thought possible. And if you had a second or third child, the miracle of that love tapping you out—again and again—but never running dry.

God's love is bigger than universes. He's got plenty to spare, and an infinite source.

For as high as the heavens are above the earth, so great is His lovingkindness toward those who fear Him. As far as the east is from the west, so far has He removed our transgressions from us.

PSALM 103:11-12

Forgiveness is a gift first given to us by Jesus, and a gift we can give ourselves. Forgiving someone does not excuse bad behavior. It simply means that you release another person from owing you anything for their mistakes.

It has been said that not forgiving someone out of spite, is like cutting yourself with a knife, trying to get another person to bleed. A graphic image. But it illustrates well that the only one unforgiveness truly hurts is the person who refuses to give it.

If you are holding back forgiveness today, try to take the courageous step of saying out loud, "I forgive _____ and release them from all responsibility for the pain they caused. I bless them in Jesus' name."

Just as the Lord forgave you,
so also should you.
COLOSSIANS 3:13

It's been said that if the entire state of Texas were covered a foot deep in quarters, JUST ONE of those quarters would represent the odds of every single Bible prophecy of Jesus coming to light. In other words, Scripture is accurate—and Jesus is a miracle.

People often say that Christmas is the most important day in the Christian calendar. And it is truly special! But the fact that Jesus, who was brutally killed—rose from death three days later...well that is the reason for victory. The cross is our hope, our salvation, and our reason for rejoicing.

For I delivered to you as of first importance what I also received, that Christ died for our sins according to the Scriptures, and that He was buried, and that He was raised on the third day according to the Scriptures.

I CORINTHIANS 15:3-4

God's timetable is not our own. He rarely can be moved to move. He is never early. He is never late. But He is always right on time.

The reason for His timing will be better understood in heaven, most likely. But we do know that He wants every single person to have the chance to receive Him. He doesn't want anyone to lose out on the chance to know Him. And for this, He is supremely patient.

Patience doesn't always (or ever!) come easily. But God is full of it, and will grow it in us by the Spirit. So hang tight and remember, there's a bigger picture. And the Master Artist is hard at work.

The Lord is not slow about His promise, as some count slowness, but is patient toward you, not wishing for any to perish but for all to come to repentance.

II PETER 3:9

You can't fight it. Or rather WHY would you want to? You've been hand-picked by the Creator of the universe to be His adopted child! And with that come all the benefits of the kingdom of heaven. You've got access to the royal treasury. You can wander the grounds or travel the world as His ambassador. And most importantly, you've got His loving ear and tender heart.

God loves each of us more than it makes sense. And He is the most generous giver of every good and perfect gift. So enjoy your special place in the family.

He chose us in Him before the foundation of the world, that we would be holy and blameless before Him.

EPHESIANS 1:4

Even the closest of relationships go through the rockiest of times. And it's in moments like these that we desperately need the truth of God's brand of love. It's a love that just won't quit. His love is full of mercy, forgiveness, and hope. It helps erase the pain and build the future.

Thankfully, God promises to give us what we need. And He cares very, very deeply about relationships. If you are in need of some healing love, just ask Him. Then wait and watch. You can believe for miraculous things.

Love...bears all things, believes all things, hopes all things, endures all things. Love never fails.

I CORINTHIANS 13:4, 7-8

In the book *The Secret Garden*, a young girl discovers a hidden passage in a wall. The passage leads to the most beautiful garden she has ever seen. And there she spends her days in wonder.

Following the Lord is like having Him lead you to secret passage after secret passage, into the most beautiful and unexpected places. Life could never be the same without Him.

It may seem convenient or simpler to do whatever feels good at the moment. But there's no simpler joy than to rest in God and let Him take you on His adventures.

Enter through the narrow gate; for the gate is wide and the way is broad that leads to destruction, and there are many who enter through it. For the gate is small and the way is narrow that leads to life, and there are few who find it.

MATTHEW 7:13-14

The call is simple: seek God with all of your heart. That's often easier said than done in the midst of challenging circumstances.

But God loves honesty, openness, and even raw feeling. He's not afraid of your tears, anger, or passion. He will just as readily dance and rejoice with you as He will to wrap you in His arms of compassion. What matters to Him is that you come to Him willingly, and willing to be broken or restored in His presence.

If you need Him in a certain area today, spend time in the Word looking for His voice to resonate with you. He may just have a very special message for your heart.

How can a young man keep his way pure?
By keeping it according to Your word.
With all my heart I have sought You; do not
let me wander from Your commandments.

PSALM 119:9-10

"She's a wild child!" the teacher says. "It's like she doesn't have any structure at home." If a child doesn't know where she stands, she's likely to act out as if in disobedience. She's looking for her freedoms and boundary lines.

As adults we tend to covet our freedom. But we are built for boundary lines too. Truly, we are safest and happiest when we know where we stand with God!

In David's time, a shepherd would create a pen in the meadow for his sheep, with a very small entrance. He would sleep across the entrance of the pen to protect them from predators. In a similar way, we are like sheep protected by our Shepherd. His boundaries keep us free and content in His presence.

The law of the LORD is perfect, restoring the soul; the testimony of the LORD is sure, making wise the simple. The precepts of the LORD are right, rejoicing the heart; the commandment of the LORD is pure, enlightening the eyes.

PSALM 19:7-8

A hurricane force wind comes at you through the telephone lines. "We'll discuss options at our next visit," the doctor explains. But through the numbness you just think about your family...your spouse...your life about to turn upside down.

There are times when the only thing to do is retreat. Not into solitude—it's the closeness of God that we most need when we're most overwhelmed. Psalm 61:2 says, "From the end of the earth I call to You when my heart is faint; Lead me to the rock that is higher than I." Only God can take us to a place of grace, where we can get through some storms.

My soul takes refuge in You;
and in the shadow of Your wings I will take
refuge until destruction passes by.

PSALM 57:1

The college kid regularly sneaks away from his dorm. His roommates don't know where he goes; they just know he's not at their parties and he's gone for an hour or two at a time. One day, a roommate notices him sneak something under his coat as he goes. As roommates do, he grabs the item from under his friend's arm. "A Bible?" The kid shrugs. "It's kind of a private thing."

Having a personal relationship with God is essential. It's also nothing to be ashamed of! In fact, knowing the Lord should be the very best news of your life! Not that it's necessary to stand on street corners or become a pastor (although both are just fine). But live your faith in a way that makes people notice a difference. Jesus did!

"Let him who boasts boast of this, that he understands and knows Me, that I am the LORD who exercises lovingkindness, justice and righteousness on earth; for I delight in these things," declares the LORD.

JEREMIAH 9:24

Chop a limb off a tree, and it won't take long to notice a difference in that limb. It will become dry and broken, leaves withered, and eventually break down back into the earth.

Now graft a branch into a tree, and you'll see a difference too. When done correctly, a grafted branch takes on the characteristics of the tree. It grows leaves and blooms, bearing fruit, and in every way acting like it belonged to that tree from the beginning.

Jesus is the vine and we are the branches. We have everything we need to bear much fruit in Him. We just need to stay connected.

I am the vine, you are the branches;
he who abides in Me and I in him,
he bears much fruit, for apart from Me
you can do nothing.

JOHN 15:5

Before a child grows up and learns to be more self-aware, smiles and laughs are a regular part of his day. Adults have a funny habit of making the strangest faces, doing everything they can to coax that baby grin to the surface. In their innocence, babies understand joy!

That shouldn't change as we get older. Knowing God, understanding Him better, and receiving His love should lead to deeper and deeper joy. The kind that can't be shaken under any circumstances.

God loves fun! Read Nehemiah 8:10 and Zephaniah 3:17 today. And find strength in His joy.

So I commended pleasure,
for there is nothing good for a man under
the sun except to eat and to drink and to be
merry, and this will stand by him in his toils
throughout the days of his life which God
has given him under the sun.

ECCLESIASTES 8:15

Traveling to a foreign country can be an interesting experience. Especially in those countries where other religions thrive. A woman was nervous about traveling to Thailand, where Buddhism reigns. She worried about the spiritual influence and how it would affect her. Would she still be able to enjoy her vacation?

But a funny thing happened. Every time she passed a Buddhist temple, she found herself praising and thanking Jesus out loud. "Oh Jesus you're here! You're welcome here! Thank You for coming with me!"

It's true that light always conquers darkness, not the other way around. When the Holy Spirit lives in us, we take Him everywhere we go!

Therefore we also have as our ambition,
whether at home or absent,
to be pleasing to Him.

II CORINTHIANS 5:9

*S*heep spend their lives in sheeply bliss. They are very flock- and family-oriented. They eat, wander, and follow whatever is in front of them!

Meanwhile, the shepherd does the heavy lifting. He watches for predators and protects the flock. If one sheep wanders too far, he goes after it. He makes sure his sheep have plenty of food, water, rest, and comfort.

In a spiritual sense, we are constantly in the presence of the Shepherd. That means we never, never have to worry about being alone or unprotected, if we keep our eye on Him. When we stray, He comes to find us. He knows the sounds of our desperate cries, and we instinctively know the sound of His voice.

He makes me lie down in green pastures;
He leads me beside quiet waters.
He restores my soul; He guides me in
the paths of righteousness for His name's sake.

PSALM 23:2-3

Knowing you are trusted can be one of the best feelings in the world. From little girls telling secrets on the playground, to the highest government officials—we understand the power of confidence and trust.

So, how does it feel to know that you have the ear and the trust of your heavenly Father? That the God of the universe reveals His mysteries to you as you build your relationship with Him? In this way, life truly is like a treasure hunt of discovery. Like babies wandering through the grass looking for the plastic eggs that Grandma has hidden, we get to enjoy and explore all the treasures of heaven when we know God.

The secret of the LORD is for those who fear Him, and He will make them know His covenant.

PSALM 25:14

The ways of the kingdom are not like the ways of the world. God always has His eye on the faithful ones, and we can trust in His reward.

It doesn't always seem fair to see people prosper when they live outside of the will of God. But it's not always with earthly things that God blesses His children.

Following Jesus is success, in the eyes of the kingdom (Matthew 6:19-21). You may not always see the size of your treasure house, but you can rest assured that His children are well taken care of.

Adversity pursues sinners, but the righteous will be rewarded with prosperity.
PROVERBS 13:21

If you've spent time at a church where the senior pastor has a family and children, you know that his kids are well known. A pastor's kid often has more access to the building and more leeway with the staff. A toddler may even wander onto the stage while her dad is preaching, and the congregation will generally have a good snicker about it. Because everyone knows who the pastor's children are.

You are a child of the King. You have access to places that many do not. The King will always make time for you and let you sit on His lap during meetings. He is keenly interested in your comings and goings. And people know who your Father is!

Because he has loved Me, therefore I will deliver him; I will set him securely on high, because he has known My name. He will call upon Me, and I will answer him; I will be with him in trouble; I will rescue him and honor him.

PSALM 91:14-15

*L*oving God means living in a way that, if your life is scrutinized, no fault will be found. Anything done in secret can be wonderful assets if your integrity is discovered when the lights are turned on. But if what is done when no one looks would expose unhealthy or sinful things—now is the time to lift those things up to God and ask for His help and guidance. After all, He already knows. He's not surprised. And He wants freedom and life for you, even more than you want it for yourself. So lay your hang-ups at His feet today, and see what good He can make of it—because He can.

Make it your ambition to lead a quiet life and attend to your own business and work with your hands, just as we commanded you, so that you will behave properly toward outsiders and not be in any need.

I THESSALONIANS 4:11-12

A man regularly had bad dreams, and he asked the Lord what to do about it. Shortly after asking, the man dreamed again. This time, while dreaming, he was able to speak out the name of Jesus. "Jesus!" At that moment the suffocating feeling in his dream disappeared. The trouble vanished. And he woke up knowing the Lord had given him a powerful weapon.

The name of Jesus saves. He heals. He restores. He redeems. He removes obstacles and delivers victory. The next time you feel desperate, helpless, or hopeless—declare the name of Jesus and see what happens.

> The name of the LORD is a strong tower;
> the righteous runs into it and is safe.
>
> PROVERBS 18:10

It can be so hard to wait. Never mind the waiting room, long lines of traffic, or a much anticipated letter in the mail. When the waiting we're doing is on God, it can seem like forever! And how do we handle it when the answer is one we didn't want? Well, think about this. An answer from God means that the God of the universe is in relationship with us! He cares enough to hear our hearts and respond. What a beautiful thing—God's "no" may be a no, but it still shows His closeness and love.

> The mind of man plans his way,
> but the LORD directs his steps.
>
> PROVERBS 16:9

A couple had just moved into a home in a new city. They had decided to finance the home and throw away their moving boxes—this was going to be forever!

Three months later, the man got a job offer in another state—the state where the woman's family lived. The woman found out she was pregnant with their first child. Suddenly, priorities shifted!

They were nervous about losing money on the sale of their new home. But the woman knew it would only take one person and the Lord. Sure enough, one man came. He returned with his wife and family. And the home sold just like that.

Need a miracle? Listen to the testimonies of others. The Lord is always up to the impossible!

With respect to the promise of God, [Abraham] did not waver in unbelief but grew strong in faith, giving glory to God, and being fully assured that what God had promised, He was able also to perform.

ROMANS 4:20-21

There are times you may find yourself in a situation where you're not clearly hearing an answer from God. That may be because He's waiting on you! God loves the partnership He has with His children, and sometimes He "leads from the back of the room"—by letting us learn through making decisions.

If you find yourself wondering, try asking the Lord if He's giving you room to grow. Then check your heart and motivations. Fast and pray. Spend time in the Word, and go for it! God will be with you if you want Him there.

Therefore Jesus, lifting up His eyes and seeing that a large crowd was coming to Him, said to Philip, "Where are we to buy bread, so that these may eat?" This He was saying to test him, for He Himself knew what He was intending to do.

JOHN 6:5-6

There are times in the Bible where it says *The Lord remembered her in her distress*, or God remembered them and acted. It's not that God forgets. But remembering can be like acknowledging a person at a certain point in time.

God knows your every need and your every move. We, on the other hand, don't always remember God! But we have a promise. If we cry out to Him and seek Him, He will be there. He will help. Sometimes, though, we need to take the first step to get out of our emotions and self-centeredness. Remember God, and He will remember you.

The righteous cry, and the LORD hears and delivers them out of all their troubles.

PSALM 34:17

There is a fairy tale about a king named Midas, who turned anything he touched into gold. At first it was a fun game. And then he hugged his daughter, and...suddenly, gold was less valuable than his princess!

The fairy tale had an unpleasant lesson. But a touch from God is a powerful thing. When He touches us, we can be moved deeply. We can be healed or feel His love in amazing ways. The Bible mentions faithful people who laid hands on the sick or those who needed a touch.

God does amazing things through His people. We can participate by being sensitive to what He is up to in any given moment and being willing to let Him use us.

And when the men of that place recognized Him, they sent word into all that surrounding district and brought to Him all who were sick; and they implored Him that they might just touch the fringe of His cloak; and as many as touched it were cured.

MATTHEW 14:35-36

There are many benefits of being a child of God. We're probably not truly aware of more than five percent of His presence in our lives! What if that detour on the road, actually detoured you away from a bad accident? What if missing your flight meant striking up a valuable conversation with a fellow delayed traveler? What if going to that other grocery store on a whim, put you in line to bless a sweet older woman to carry her groceries out?

God works in many amazing, some obvious, and usually subtle ways. The more we open our eyes, the more He opens our eyes. And we begin to see the true beauty of the world around us.

When you pass through the waters, I will be with you; and through the rivers, they will not overflow you. When you walk through the fire, you will not be scorched, nor will the flame burn you. Do not fear, for I am with you; I will bring your offspring from the east, and gather you from the west.

ISAIAH 43:2, 5

The elderly are full of rich wisdom. Their experience on earth surpasses any other people you interact with on a daily basis. They may not always recognize it—but the elderly are treasure troves of stories, examples, and advice to younger people.

Not many folks love wrinkles and saggy skin. But the Lord appreciates the wisdom that wrinkles represent. Proverbs 61:31 makes that clear, calling grey hair a crown of glory coming from a godly life.

So if you're aging (as we all are), own it! You're beautiful, and your wisdom is growing day by day.

Therefore we do not lose heart,
but though our outer man is decaying,
yet our inner man is being renewed
day by day.
II CORINTHIANS 4:16

The religious mindset says, "There are rules you must follow in order to be loved." The relationship mindset says, "Love God and be loved by Him, and you'll have delight for His ways."

The simple truth is, believe in your heart that Jesus is Lord, and confess Him with your lips. That's all it takes to be in relationship with Him. All the details will fall into place as we get to know Him.

So just believe. Scared today? Lonely? Confused? Just believe He is who He says He is. Confirm it through His word. Believe, and it will all work out in the end.

Truly, truly, I say to you, he who hears My word, and believes Him who sent Me, has eternal life, and does not come into judgment, but has passed out of death into life.

JOHN 5:24

A little girl would pray the same prayer every night before bed: "God, please mark FORGIVEN on all the things I've done wrong up in my book in heaven."

Her theology was a bit off, but she had the right idea! Forgiveness is the Lord's specialty. And He has something written about you in heaven! But it's not a list of sins. Those are erased at the time of forgiveness. What God *does* know is your name, once you've accepted Jesus. You are indelibly marked as a chosen child, and nothing can steal that away.

Nevertheless do not rejoice in this,
that the spirits are subject to you,
but rejoice that your names
are recorded in heaven.

LUKE 10:20

Your job is about to be sabotaged. Your boss wants you out, and she's winning. She has lied about you and made you look terrible, and that is getting you fired.

You can fight. You can go to HR. You can make a list of all the ways your boss is a terrible human being. But God says, *Be still.*

Can you do it? Can you lay down your sword, trust in His plan, and allow Him to do the fighting?

The end result may not be what you want or expect...or it may be even better. But God is just. He always wins. And that energy it would take to fight, it can be put to use in resting in His embrace as He goes to battle for you.

> *The LORD will fight for you*
> *while you keep silent.*
>
> EXODUS 14:14

They might be big. They might be scary. They might be downright mean. But no matter what, bullies are just people with bristles. And all people are powerless in the presence of God.

The Lord is the only forever-lasting Person there is. No one but He can determine your path. And He has power over the people who would manipulate you or feed on fear.

First, remember Whom you truly serve. Remember His absolute authority. And then pray in peace. He will determine the course of your life, no matter what others may think, say, or do.

I, even I, am He who comforts you. Who are you that you are afraid of man who dies and of the son of man who is made like grass, that you have forgotten the LORD your Maker, Who stretched out the heavens and laid the foundations of the earth, that you fear continually all day long because of the fury of the oppressor, as he makes ready to destroy? But where is the fury of the oppressor?

ISAIAH 51:12–13

You've probably heard a phrase similar to this: The road to destruction is paved with good intentions. In other words, it's very easy to imagine doing a good thing, and quite another to actually follow through.

We are human, after all. Imperfect, messy, gloriously beautiful humans who need the grace of God. We also sometimes need to be reminded of *why* we need Him.

Don't be discouraged if you fail, even if you meant well. Instead, that's a great opportunity to remember your humanness and thank the Lord for His mercy. Ask for His forgiveness. Then get up and try again. He is, after all, the God of second chances.

But he said to Him, "Lord, with You I am ready to go both to prison and to death!" And He said, "I say to you, Peter, the rooster will not crow today until you have denied three times that you know Me."

LUKE 22:33-34

The Christian life is full of chain reactions. And God always goes first. We love, because He first loved us (1 Jn. 4:19). We forgive, just as He forgave us (Eph. 4:32). Every one of our experiences can be used to encourage, teach, or train others who are experiencing what we did. Our hardships, and how the Lord gets us through them, give us empathy for others going through similar things.

Jesus is constantly interceding for us before the throne of our Father. We can follow suit and pray for others.

Who has come to your mind today? A neighbor or family member? A missionary or the mail carrier? Spend a few minutes asking God how you can pray for them, just as Jesus prays for you.

Simon, Simon, behold, Satan has demanded permission to sift you like wheat; but I have prayed for you, that your faith may not fail; and you, when once you have turned again, strengthen your brothers.

LUKE 22:31-32

She had been a straight "A" student in high school, but college seemed to be falling to bits. She comes home smelling like smoke, pierced and tattooed, refusing to participate in family activities. That smile you used to adore hasn't been seen on her face for a long time. *What happened to my baby*, you wonder.

God's love is the best. Better even than a parent's love for their children. His heart breaks when we turn away, and He rejoices when we accept His love with open arms.

We have the choice to remain in God's love. His heart is always wide open. He patiently waits if we turn away from Him. But it always feels best to accept His love and stay there.

> Just as the Father has loved Me,
> I have also loved you; abide in My love.
>
> JOHN 15:9

*H*ow can laundry, cleaning up kid messes, and trying not to yell at the twins be my calling, she wonders hopelessly. Life sometimes feels like a mess, not a ministry. But the Lord loves her work. He grins when she gets down on the ground and plays with her sons and their action figures. His heart fills every time she folds her husband's shirts and puts them away. Because ultimately, He knows her heart. And she doesn't do life perfectly, but she does her best to love the Lord well through it all.

> *Whatever you do in word or deed,*
> *do all in the name of the Lord Jesus,*
> *giving thanks through Him to God the Father.*
> COLOSSIANS 3:17

Nick Vujicic was born without limbs. His parents decided to raise him to believe he could do anything. His growing up years were not easy, but Nick now has an international ministry of hope and encouragement.

Each of us gets to choose how we view our own circumstances. *Have I gotten the short end of the stick? Or will I allow my personal challenges to grow me? Will I allow Jesus to shine through the cracks in my armor, for the benefit of the world around me?*

Jesus promised that the world was full of trouble. He also promised that He has overcome the world. So, do we look at the trouble, or look to the Victor? The choice is up to each of us.

Stripes that wound scour away evil,
and strokes reach the innermost parts.

PROVERBS 20:30

He was too short to see over crowds of heads. Besides, everyone hated him. So it's not like they would make a path for him to get up front. But he *had* to see. He'd heard about this man who seemed to love everyone and spoke so wisely. So he climbed a tree and peered out from the leaves.

Then the unthinkable happened. The celebrity somehow spotted Zach through the foliage. "Hey! Hey Zacchaeus!" I'm coming over today with my friends. We want to hang out with you. It'll be great!"

Jesus knows you. He knows me. And He tends to be drawn to the ones who feel most invisible and most hungry. So lean in and show your interest. He'll certainly catch your eye.

Are not two sparrows sold for a cent? And yet not one of them will fall to the ground apart from your Father. So do not fear; you are more valuable than many sparrows.

MATTHEW 10:29, 31

The drippy mess sits there on the sidewalk, sagging as it melts in the springtime sun. Above the blob, a small hand. In the hand, an empty ice cream cone. Above the cone, a quivering lip and two doe eyes filling to the brim as they search your face in despair.

Are you angry that your 4-year-old dropped her ice cream? Will you scold her for being careless? Or does your heart melt just a little bit along with that strawberry mess, as you take your daughter's hand and head back to the parlor for a fresh scoop—maybe in a cup this time?

God's mercy is indescribable, and His tolerance so merciful. He loves our innocence, and understands our current level of maturity.

Just as a father has compassion on his children, so the LORD has compassion on those who fear Him. For He Himself knows our frame; He is mindful that we are but dust.

PSALM 103:13-14

Sometime, open your Bible to Isaiah chapter 6 and then Revelation 1:12-16. Try to put yourself in the shoes of the writers who observed the Lord in His splendor and majesty. Imagine being there, experiencing such strange and awe-filled moments.

Sometime, find a way to watch a sunrise uninterrupted. Watch the colors form and grow over the horizon. Or go whale watching. Or watch an infant sleeping peacefully.

What we see now is just a glimpse of His true glory. But imagine the day when we won't have to imagine at all—we will be in His presence forever.

Bless the LORD, O my soul!
O LORD my God, You are very great;
You are clothed with splendor and majesty.

PSALM 104:1

Sometimes things happen just so God can show us who He really is. Sometimes we end up in situations that are tailor made for our cries out to Him for help and understanding. Then when He delivers, it's so obvious where the help came from!

How often do people forget to call on God in times of need? How often do we try to do things under our own steam, only to give up defeated and exhausted?

The next time you find yourself striving, try dropping everything and crying out to Him. He may just have the answer you've been waiting for.

*Now, O LORD our God, I pray,
deliver us from his hand that all the kingdoms
of the earth may know that You alone,
O LORD, are God.*

II KINGS 19:19

Do you know how strong you are? Do you truly realize what you're capable of? Probably, most people don't know until they find themselves stretched to the limit. A mother experiences this as she gives birth. At the point of no return, the lion within roars up and surprises the victor!

"Not by might, nor by power, but by My Spirit," says the Lord (Zech. 4:6). Those who believe in Jesus have the same power that raised Him from the dead living in them. That's why when Jesus says that nothing will be impossible for those who believe, we can trust He knows what He's talking about.

From the days of John the Baptist until now the kingdom of heaven suffers violence, and violent men take it by force.

MATTHEW 11:12

We were made to belong to a community of believers. There are many reasons for this, but one is because it can be so encouraging to hear and witness the ways God works through others. Encouraging and loving others not only strengthens the community and ourselves, but it also makes room for God to tip His cup of blessing into you to fill you up again!

With God, your cup never runs dry. The more you pour out, the more He pours in. As long as you're following His lead, He will build you up as you strengthen those around you.

But you, beloved, building yourselves up
on your most holy faith,
praying in the Holy Spirit.

JUDE 20

God is in the miracle business. Not just in distant, news-making headline ways. And not just in other people. *You*, friend, are a walking miracle. If you've accepted Christ, then you are a new creation. The old you, replaced. The old sin, erased. The devil's work, disgraced by Jesus who took on your brokenness and released you from darkness. Nothing can change it. You didn't do anything to earn it. He just loves you. A lot.

People may show off pictures of their grandkids, or talk about their new car or job or house or latest accomplishment. All of that is fine, of course. But the truest joy, the greatest accomplishment wasn't made by you or me. It was Jesus. And *that* is news worth spreading.

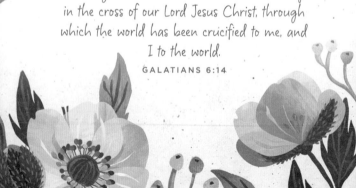

But may it never be that I would boast, except
in the cross of our Lord Jesus Christ, through
which the world has been crucified to me, and
I to the world.

GALATIANS 6:14

There were two trees in the garden. One, off-limits. One, full of life. In fact, the whole rest of the garden was at their fingertips...except the single tree.

Of course, we are a curious bunch. A "but why not *that* one" kind of people. And so, the falling. The breaking. The "let's try this again, but this time there are serious rules to keep you on track" situation.

But nothing, apart from grace, can get us close enough. No one but Jesus can take us to the Father. So, He made a way.

God is glorious and untouchable, tender and compassionate. And by His grace, we belong right by His side.

The Law came in so that the transgression would increase; but where sin increased, grace abounded all the more.

ROMANS 5:20

She was a lowlife. A scumbag. A prostitute. A prostitute for *priests*, no less. But she recognized the work of God when she saw it. So Rahab helped the Israelite scouts to escape, and they promised to return the favor.

So when the city was destroyed, Rahab and her family were rescued. She married an Israelite. And Rahab is listed in the genealogy of Jesus.

God doesn't look at the situation so much as He looks at the heart. A pure and open heart can receive truth. Ask Him to reveal anything blocking your view today...and keep your eyes open for His work in the world around you.

(God) raised us up with Him, and seated us with Him in the heavenly places in Christ Jesus, so that in the ages to come He might show the surpassing riches of His grace in kindness toward us in Christ Jesus.

EPHESIANS 2:6-7

Try this experiment. Have a friend stand five feet away from you and toss a beach ball in your direction. Can you catch it? Most likely! Now have him stand twenty feet away and toss a baseball hard enough for you to catch it. But wait! Put on a blindfold first. *Yikes!*

It helps so much to see what's coming. It helps to keep your eye on the one who knows where it's coming from too. Stay tuned in to the Lord, and you'll have the sense of peace that comes from knowing you can trust Him. Turn your eyes toward your circumstances, and you'll more than likely experience anxiety and fear of the unknown.

The steadfast of mind You will keep in perfect peace, because he trusts in You.

ISAIAH 26:3

If only we could see into the future. *Far* into the future, into the heavens, into eternity. If we could understand what eternal life with the Lord will be like, we probably wouldn't think twice about the things that worry us today. The fast food meal we crave would taste like dust compared to the table set before us. The movie with the questionable rating wouldn't even get our second glance.

The things of heaven can't truly be imagined, planned for, or measured. But we can dream. And thank Him in advance for choosing us as His heavenly kids.

Blessed be the God and
Father of our Lord Jesus Christ,
who has blessed us with every spiritual
blessing in the heavenly places in Christ.
EPHESIANS 1:3

It's hard to imagine, without experiencing it, the peace that comes from trusting God with every detail of life. The news and social media don't exactly reflect a life of peace and trust! But little by little, as we learn to lean on God as our Shepherd, our trust in Him grows. We start to apply past circumstances to our current situation, knowing He can come through this time like He did the last. We listen to others share their stories. And we learn to let go.

It's countercultural and weird to some. But we, as believers, are made to stand out and shine as we lean back and rest in the Lord.

The LORD is my shepherd, I shall not want.
He makes me lie down in green pastures;
He leads me beside quiet waters. He restores
my soul; He guides me in the paths of
righteousness for His name's sake.

PSALM 23:1-3

Every person on the planet is kind of like a seed. A potential-packed package that needs the right environment to grow. Many, many of these seeds stay unplanted, or planted in toxic soil. Others stay in their window trays, never reaching their full impact.

But there are some that take to the soil and take root. They weather the winters, suck up the springtime rain, share fruit in the summer, and lose leaves in the fall. These seed-people have discovered that the Master Gardener knows what He's doing, pruning shears and all. And for that they will bear fruit the rest of their lives.

For you were continually straying like sheep, but now you have returned to the Shepherd and Guardian of your souls.

I PETER 2:25

*L*ife with Jesus is not like a punch card at the office. You can't wear a sign that says "Jesus is In" or "Jesus is At Lunch—Back By 1:00." He is with you 24/7. In the dark and in the daytime. While you sleep and while you run errands. He's a companion of the most loyal sort.

You are never alone. Not in a creepy "someone is watching you" sort of way! But in the way that, no matter what you need, you have a Source to turn to. You have the Answer at your fingertips. And you have the power to accomplish all things in Christ.

> When I awake,
> I am still with You.
>
> PSALM 139:18

It is said of dangerous influences, like drugs, that a person is never satisfied. Addicts' lives are built around getting the next hit. It is an empty, goal-less existence.

In a completely opposite, upside-down way, the kingdom of God is full of very hungry people. The difference is, once you taste His goodness, you are both instantly satisfied and instantly hungry for more of Him! And it never stops! God honors our passion and hunger. If we seek, He promises we will find. And to those who ask, He gives.

So bring your hunger to the Lord. And you will be satisfied, over and over again, for the rest of your days.

The apostles said to the Lord,
"Increase our faith!"
LUKE 17:5

This is a *right now* culture. Unlike our parents' and grandparents' generations, meals that take longer than 30 minutes to cook are almost unheard of. And just imagine waiting more than 5 minutes for a burger at the nearest fast food restaurant. Waiting is not a gift that comes naturally to most of us!

But God's world is a *patience* culture. There is so much to look forward to, far beyond anything we could dare to ask or imagine. There will be a day when His faithful people will be rewarded beyond belief.

It just means that now, we wait. We live. Get to know Him as He is, follow faithfully, love others, and dream of the life to come. Just know this—it's going to be *good!*

He will set you high above all nations which He has made, for praise, fame, and honor; and that you shall be a consecrated people to the LORD your God, as He has spoken.

DEUTERONOMY 26:19

What does generosity look like to you? Is it the wealthy benefactor who gives a million dollars to the orphan's fund? Or the homeless man who shares half of his meal with a disabled friend? Are you ever challenged by other people's generosity—or are you the one who sets the bar for others?

The Lord looks not at the outside, but at the heart of a person. So whatever all out means to you—being sold out and willing to give whatever blesses the Lord—that is what pleases *His* heart.

It may not be money. It may be time, hope, or service. Whatever you feel to give in His name. That is generosity of a kingdom sort.

Calling His disciples to Him, He said to them, "Truly I say to you, this poor widow put in more than all the contributors to the treasury; for they all put in out of their surplus, but she, out of her poverty, put in all she owned, all she had to live on."

MARK 12:43-44

When a relationship is broken, it can be the most painful and heart wrenching experience. The Lord values relationships so highly, and feels the pain or joy of them very deeply. He allows us to experience brokenness. But only because He is the Master of restoration.

If you've never experienced such conflict that you are desperate for the Lord's intervention, you can count your blessings! On the other hand, if you *have* needed His restoration, and finally received it—you know how sweet it is. Restoration is beautiful. It draws two people closer together; wiser and stronger. And it showcases one of His very best gifts—hope and healing in His people.

He has made everything appropriate
in its time. He has also set eternity
in their heart, yet so that man will not find out
the work which God has done from
the beginning even to the end.

ECCLESIASTES 3:11

"Oh, here she comes! She's coming!" one exclaims. The crowd erupts in cheers. Music begins playing joyfully from the air. Flags wave, streamers stream, confetti gathers on the street. And she, in her white robe, face beaming with joy, enters into her reward with a bounding dance.

She pauses only when a figure comes into view. Tall and gleaming, the look on His face is the purest love. She runs forward into an embrace. He tucks her into His arms. "Welcome home, beloved."

On this side of heaven, losing loved ones is hard. But for those who love God the reward is outstanding. Earth life traded for eternal life. Death may seem hard for us, but to God, it is the beginning of rebirth.

Precious in the sight of the LORD
is the death of His godly ones.

PSALM 116:15

It's not cruelty. It's not exclusivity. Jesus honestly, openly welcomes anyone who acknowledges Him as Lord and believes. No other faith group has such a policy of love. "Come. *Please* come. Just believe—take a tiny step of faith in My direction—and you'll see!" He patiently waits for any willing heart to look His way. He pursues His chosen people.

Jesus isn't looking for mindless, soulless followers who blindly say yes to every command. He wants people to see the options—both good and bad—and still choose Him. Not because He is proud, but because He loves. And He wants His beloved to thrive.

Jesus said to him, "I am the way, and the truth, and the life; no one comes to the Father but through Me."

JOHN 14:6

Before you knew Him, you had to do it all. Alone. You functioned under your own power, created your own guidance, listened to anything that sounded good to you, and built your own truth.

After choosing Him, you became a dwelling place for God! He never leaves you or leaves you alone. Your greatest power is His power in you. Holy Spirit guides, comforts, and supports you. The Word is your food and the best source of Wisdom and truth.

Life before Jesus can't truly be compared with life after. You were once a caterpillar, crawling and eating. Now you are a butterfly, a thing of real beauty. A new creation in Christ.

Jesus said to her, "I am the resurrection and the life; he who believes in Me will live even if he dies, and everyone who lives and believes in Me will never die. Do you believe this?"

JOHN 11:25-26

The drought has lasted for seven years. As a missionary in Africa, you've seen countless villagers die.

One day you stumble upon a camp you've never seen before. It is deserted; the inhabitants have left it all behind. Each tent is filled with salted meats, fruits, and jugs of water.

So, what do you do? Erase your footprints and hide it all away? No! You run, yelling, back to the village! *"We've been saved! We have hope! Our God is amazing!"*

The truth of Jesus is just that good. Worth shouting from rooftops, to the spiritually hungry all over the world. So go! Share! Even if it's just with one person today.

For I am not ashamed of the gospel, for it is the power of God for salvation to everyone who believes, to the Jew first and also to the Greek.

ROMANS 1:16

Sometimes we expect God to show up in a certain way for us, but He's not there. Other times, He shows up in ways that we least expect.

God doesn't fit in a box (or a tomb, for that matter). Nothing can hold Him back from unfolding His perfect plan. We don't often have angels showing up and clearing up our confusion. So the best thing we can do is train ourselves to discover Him where He chooses to be seen.

The Lord speaks uniquely to each of us. As you learn who He is to you, how He communicates will become clearer. And you'll learn to love the way He invades your circumstances—whether you expect Him to or not.

The angel said to the women, "Do not be afraid; for I know that you are looking for Jesus who has been crucified. He is not here, for He has risen, just as He said. Come, see the place where He was lying."

MATTHEW 28:5-6

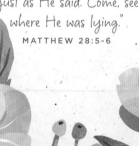

I would die for you, the love song croons on the radio. *I would cross oceans just to be with you.* A skeptic listens to that and thinks, *really? I mean really.*

It's hard to imagine a passion so deep, a loyalty so strong that a person would put his life on the line for another. But it's been done. It's the reason we have hope.

Because our Father made the ultimate sacrifice of His Son—and the Son made the ultimate sacrifice of His life—we can believe that anything we need is within reach. He is the giver of the most amazing gifts—and He will stop at nothing to lavish you with His love.

He who did not spare His own Son, but delivered Him over for us all, how will He not also with Him freely give us all things?

ROMANS 8:32

She absolutely loves the smell of a fisherman's wharf. It reminds her of childhood trips to the seaside. He, on the other hand, can hardly stand to be on the same street! *Yuck!*

Whether a person likes a certain fragrance or not, the fragrance is what it is. It can be identified, because it is always the same.

And whether a person likes Jesus or not, Jesus is known. A person cannot be confronted with Him and not be changed, and a person cannot forget the impact of His influence. His presence is in us by the power of the Holy Spirit—and those who experience Him through us will never be the same.

> For we are a fragrance of Christ to God among those who are being saved and among those who are perishing.
> II CORINTHIANS 2:15

C.S. Lewis said, "There are far better things ahead than any we leave behind." It doesn't matter if you are a billionaire with a vacation home on the Sienne, or a single mother who scrapes by each month. Whatever your situation, your heavenly life will exceed all possible expectations.

That's why it pays to be generous now. Not just with money, but with your heart and life. The more we love now, the greater our treasure grows in heaven. And perhaps that gives Jesus even more to work with as He prepares your heavenly home.

In My Father's house are many dwelling places; if it were not so, I would have told you; for I go to prepare a place for you.

JOHN 14:2

Getting a new job or position is the beginning of a chapter. It can be seen as the title page in a book: *Bill Begins Work at Home Products, Inc.* But the bulk of the chapter—the story itself—gets written over time, as you immerse yourself into the company and the work. There will be high and low points, and all of it will lead to...yes, the next chapter title and the next part of the story.

The Lord often delivers us to the threshold of a new season. We may be given new opportunities. Or we may experience a new healing or deliverance. But the way those things play out in our lives take time and partnership with the Holy Spirit.

The LORD your God will clear away these nations before you little by little; you will not be able to put an end to them quickly, for the wild beasts would grow too numerous for you.

DEUTERONOMY 7:22

The Lord loves an eager student! If we look at Jesus as an example, He spent three solid years with the same twelve eager young men. Now that's commitment to a cause!

God is drawn to our hunger and willingness to learn. There's so much He can do with a pliable heart. On the other hand, a hard or prideful heart will most likely be left that way, until such time as the person decides to change.

Do a spiritual checkup of your heart today. Are you willing to learn? Are you tender and soft before God? If so, there's no limit to what He can do in and through you.

Teach me, O LORD, the way of Your statutes, and I shall observe it to the end. Give me understanding, that I may observe Your law and keep it with all my heart.

PSALM 119:33-34

God never, ever goes back on His word. If you can find a promise written, if you remember a word given, then continue to thank God for those things and believe they will happen. His timetable may not line up perfectly with yours, but His intentions will not waver.

For as many as are the promises of God, in [Jesus] they are yes! (2 Cor. 1:20) The empty tomb was a sealing of the new covenant of hope and salvation.

So take heart, friend. If you believe, you will receive every ounce of promise you've been given by a very great God.

Calling a bird of prey from the east, the man of My purpose from a far country. Truly I have spoken; truly I will bring it to pass. I have planned it, surely I will do it.

ISAIAH 46:11

There's no shame in being different. In fact, living as aliens is pretty much our calling in life! It can sometimes feel like a confusing and delicate balance to love people but not the world. It can be a struggle to know how to live in the culture but not be influenced by it.

Still, God gives us all the resources we need. And He delights in our partnership with Him to live out His love.

You may have a special preference for certain movies, books, exercise styles, or other influences. Pay attention to that. Ask the Lord if it is a worldly tendency you have, or if it is a method He wants to use in order to draw you closer to the people who need Him.

All these died in faith, without receiving the promises, but having seen them and having welcomed them from a distance, and having confessed that they were strangers and exiles on the earth. For those who say such things make it clear that they are seeking a country of their own. ...But as it is, they desire a better country, that is, a heavenly one. Therefore God is not ashamed to be called their God; for He has prepared a city for them.

HEBREWS 11:13-14, 16

Take a close look at today's Scripture. Let it really sink in. Breathe in the truth of it: *God considers you family.*

Not your loopy Aunt Sally who talks too much and kisses too hard. Not the brother you no longer speak to because of that thing you fought over 20 years ago. The Lord, our God, loves you as family He *wants* to be with. He decided you should exist, and He created you. Then He called you by name and placed you right where you belong.

Earthly family is full of strange, wonderful human dynamics. But with God it's pretty straightforward: you're loved beyond measure.

For both He who sanctifies and those who are sanctified are all from one Father; for which reason He is not ashamed to call them brethren.

HEBREWS 2:11

Heart conditions are nothing to sniff at. If one is detected in a patient, the doctor will watch it closely. People with a heart condition are often affected in breathing, energy, coloring, or other symptoms. They often change habits or lifestyle in hopes of reversing or improving the state of their heart.

The spiritual heart condition is similar! Rotten thoughts, motivations, or belief systems will show up outwardly in the way a person behaves. He can try to mask it, if he's aware. But sooner or later the true condition of his heart will come out.

If you notice behaviors or thoughts in yourself that you're not happy with, take a look at your heart with the help of Holy Spirit. He will reveal any condition in you that needs adjustment, and He will help.

You have heard that the ancients were told,
"You shall not commit murder," and "Whoever commits
murder shall be liable to the court." But I say to you
that everyone who is angry with his brother shall
be guilty before the court; and whoever says to his
brother, "You good-for-nothing," shall be guilty before
the supreme court; and whoever says, "You fool," shall
be guilty enough to go into the fiery hell.

MATTHEW 5:21-22

You are on a walk in a meadow. From high above, you see a white form float in your direction. The form draws closer—a cockatoo—and lands gently on your shoulder. It tucks its beak into your neck as you walk on.

You don't know why it is here, but you want it to stay. So, do you bounce around and yell? *No!* You walk gently. Gingerly. Extremely aware of this strange miracle.

Now imagine that what rests on you is the Holy Spirit. The most beautiful gift has chosen you as a resting place. Be aware. Sense His presence and His leading. And do all you can to help Him feel welcome with you. If you do, you'll be keeping the best company there is.

Beloved, do not believe every spirit, but test the spirits to see whether they are from God, because many false prophets have gone out into the world. By this you know the Spirit of God: every spirit that confesses that Jesus Christ has come in the flesh is from God.

1 JOHN 4:1-2

So, what's the trick to getting what we want from God? A trick question, right? Well...sort of!

God gives according to His will. He knows that His will is best for us, and we don't always see the bigger picture.

But as we draw closer to Him and allow the Holy Spirit to do His transforming work in us, then little by little our hearts change. Our desires begin to line up with His desires. And in that way, we ask what He wants of us, and He delivers.

So the question isn't about how to manipulate God. It's about how we can line ourselves up with His will, and then see blessing after blessing unfold.

This is the confidence which we have before Him, that, if we ask anything according to His will, He hears us. And if we know that He hears us in whatever we ask, we know that we have the requests which we have asked from Him.

I JOHN 5:14-15

Many times in Scripture we're told not to worry. Just don't! *But, you say, that must not apply in my situation. My son is being bullied and the teacher won't do anything...or...If my husband doesn't find work soon, we'll lose our house...Worrying must count for something...right?!?*

But when God says don't, He means it. That may feel defeating. But it should empower you! He never asks us to do what we can't, with His help.

The next time you are prone to worry, be very deliberate about choosing thanks. Think of crazy things to be thankful for. Your dining room table! Boxed hair color! Your son's tender, compassionate heart! Thanks is sometimes the very best warfare.

Do not worry then, saying, "What will we eat?" or "What will we drink?" or "What will we wear for clothing?" For the Gentiles eagerly seek all these things; for your heavenly Father knows that you need all these things.

MATTHEW 6:31-32

She struggled for many years with depression. She cried out to Jesus, and tried to follow, but doubt and fear crept in and stayed. So when her life ended, people weren't sure if it was an accident...or on purpose.

Many things are hard to understand, the pastor said at the funeral. No one knows how certain things work in the kingdom. "But," he continued, "Neither death nor life, neither angels nor demons..." Nothing can separate a child of God from His love.

No one has the big answers except the Lord. But we also know His Word is true, and He never goes back on His word. When you face big questions, remember this: It is not yours to worry. It is yours to trust, and receive His peace.

For I am convinced that neither death, nor life, nor angels, nor principalities, nor things present, nor things to come, nor powers, nor height, nor depth, nor any other created thing, will be able to separate us from the love of God, which is in Christ Jesus our Lord.

ROMANS 8:38-39

Have you ever been around someone who always seems happy? Spend enough time around them and you will notice two things: 1) You want to be around them; and 2) They're probably not always happy!

Some people have learned to tap into the deep joy of the Lord. They have truly experienced Nehemiah 8:10, that His joy is our strength. These people experience hardships and challenges. They go through tough things, but with a peace that passes understanding and with a willingness to search for the good in it all. We are drawn to this ability to see Jesus in all things.

Want to be that kind of person? Ask the Lord to lead you on a journey of joy.

A cheerful heart has a continual feast.

PROVERBS 15:15

everal years ago there was a television advertisement featuring a Jolly Green Giant and his not-so-giant son. In one of the ads, the son tries to scare birds away from the vegetables. At first the birds don't budge. And then suddenly they flee! The little son is so proud. Then he turns around to see that he is standing in the shadow of his giant dad—the true reason for the birds' escape.

You stand in the shadow of the King of Kings. Nothing can defeat you. Demons know your Father, and they are very afraid. So stand strong and wait for Him to make His move. You *will* be saved!

For after all it is only just for God
to repay with affliction those who afflict you...
dealing out retribution to those who do not
know God and to those who do not obey
the gospel of our Lord Jesus.

II THESSALONIANS 1:6, 8

Yes, he's mean. Yes, he's sneaky...sort of. He's kind of predictable. Not to mention the fact that you have access to his team's playbook, the very best spies, and a direct line to the Creator of the universe. So don't be afraid. The enemy may prowl around *like* a roaring lion, but...

"Stop weeping; behold, *the Lion* that is from the tribe of Judah, the Root of David, has overcome" (Rev. 5:5, emphasis mine). The *real* Lion is on your side! So be alert, and keep company with the One who has already overcome the world.

Be of sober spirit, be on the alert.
Your adversary, the devil, prowls around
like a roaring lion, seeking someone to devour.

I PETER 5:8

Want to end up in the pit? It's easy! Just think you're the coolest cat in town. Assume you know better. Tell them you have more experience and should be listened to. Expect others to respect you, and if they don't, get mad.

If the pit doesn't sound so fun, then try this. Take the last seat at the table, or better yet, stand. Ask how you can help. Bend over backwards to love the unlovable. Apologize first. Listen well. Make the other person feel valued.

Jesus had every right to strut His stuff. But He washed their feet instead. The best way for *you* to be honored by God, is to follow His example and take the lowest position.

Pride goes before destruction,
and a haughty spirit before stumbling.
PROVERBS 16:18

"It's just one ship, we can take it!" The soldier peered through a tiny crack and made out what he saw. But his comrade said, "Stand up and look over the fence with me." When the soldier stepped away from his limited view and looked from a higher positon, he saw an entire fleet heading in their direction.

Your view is most certainly limited, along with everyone else's. But your fellow believers are seeing things from *their* perspective. So if you put both perspectives together, the two of you...or three, or four...will understand things on a whole new level. Assume others have a piece of the puzzle you could benefit from, and you'll certainly become wiser for it.

Do nothing from selfishness or empty conceit, but with humility of mind regard one another as more important than yourselves.

PHILIPPIANS 2:3

School teachers and medical doctors have something in common: continuing education. If a doctor stopped learning in med school, then twenty years later her knowledge would fall short of the newer diseases and treatments. Things could get dangerous, fast!

Staying connected to the Source of all knowledge and wisdom is a must for believers. He is generous with what He has. But you have to be in a position to receive. If you do, you'll bear the sweetest, most helpful fruit.

Get and stay in tune with the Holy Spirit, your glue for remaining in the Vine.

Abide in Me, and I in you. As the branch cannot bear fruit of itself unless it abides in the vine, so neither can you unless you abide in Me.

JOHN 15:4

*S*in doesn't begin when a person *does* the wrong thing. It begins when the idea or feeling knocks on the door of her heart and she chooses to entertain it.

Much like a baby, sin is conceived. It takes not just the seed idea, but also a place to take root. That's where your power lies. You can refuse the seed. You can take captive that thought and kick it out the window of your heart.

Be nasty about it! Strap on the football gear. Hunker down and play linebacker with your thoughts! You're the only one that can kill sin at the root. Ask the Holy Spirit to run interference for you. And run to win.

But each one is tempted when he is carried away and enticed by his own lust. Then when lust has conceived, it gives birth to sin; and when sin is accomplished, it brings forth death.

JAMES 1:14-15

A wise pastor once said, if you don't run into a demon now and then as you are walking, then you and the demons may be heading in the same direction. Sounds kind of harsh! But the idea is solid. The devil isn't scared of people who aren't fighting for the kingdom. He's fine with complacent, lukewarm hearts. But he hates humble hearts full of passion for Jesus. Because he knows we're dangerous.

If you're not encountering opposition as you go, then check your direction. Align yourself with the Word and with Jesus. Then be thankful when challenges come. That means you're doing good things for and with God!

Woe to you when all men speak well of you, for their fathers used to treat the false prophets in the same way.

LUKE 6:26

The hardest, most essential part we play happens in our minds and hearts. It is to simply believe.

This may sound *too* easy! But try putting your faith into practice when all the hard things come. When the atheist neighbor gets your dream job. When a man in a wheelchair passes you on the street after you've just read about laying hands on a person and seeing them instantly healed. Belief can be unbelievably hard!

But your belief should not be in yourself. Your belief should be in Jesus, the One who *can* and *will* work through you. He is looking for the faithful few who will take a step of belief. Will that be you today?

Therefore they said to Him, "What shall we do, so that we may work the works of God?" Jesus answered and said to them, "This is the work of God, that you believe in Him whom He has sent."

JOHN 6:28-29

Some of the action movies today have incredible weapons: Huge things that wipe out entire cities or make people disappear.

It's hard to imagine that we have access to weapons even more powerful than the fantasy ones on television, or even the ones used by the armed forces today. But we do!

Our most powerful weapons don't look dangerous at all. They look like adoring Jesus in worship. Thankfulness, encouragement, choosing not to be offended, and praying at all times, in every way, are all weapons against the devil.

The devil doesn't want us to understand our power, so he tries to undermine our knowledge. Keep alert, and keep loving with all the strength you have.

The weapons of our warfare are not of the flesh, but divinely powerful for the destruction of fortresses.

II CORINTHIANS 10:4

As defined in Webster's dictionary (1828), *rejoice* means to "experience joy and gladness in a high degree; to be exhilarated with lively and pleasurable sensations; to exult." Wow, what a life we're expected to lead! One with high levels of joy and gladness, with exhilaration and pleasure mixed in. Not too shabby!

If you're like most people, most of your life is not lived at a high level of exhilaration. So many distractions and opportunities to worry. So much hurt.

Only the grace of God can bring us to a place where rejoicing is an everyday, every moment way of life. But it *is* possible. Because He says so. If you want to live a rejoicing life, ask Him to show you the way. Sooner than you think, you'll be dancing.

Rejoice in the Lord always;
again I will say, rejoice!
PHILIPPIANS 4:4

As you grow closer to the Lord, the relationship gets sweeter and sweeter. There may come a point where death—the world's most feared outcome—seems more like a happy gateway into the most wonderful outcome there is.

But at the same time, as your heart grows more and more like Jesus, you see the desperate need around you. Compassion levels soar. Your heart breaks for the world's brokenness. And you ache to serve in a way that makes a difference.

God's plans for you are perfect, and not one day—this side of heaven or the other—will be stolen from you. Love hard now, and you will most certainly receive the faithful servant's reward.

For to me, to live is Christ and to die is gain...
But I am hard-pressed from both directions,
having the desire to depart and be with Christ,
for that is very much better.

PHILIPPIANS 1:21, 23

One daughter takes what she wants. She scrabbles around for goodies and sweets, grabs the toys she wants to play with, and assumes that when she wants to go to the park instead of to school it will happen.

Another daughter waits to receive. She appreciates a full plate and a balanced day. On occasion, she asks kindly if a treat might be had after dinner, or a picnic might be a nice way to spend a Saturday.

God's heart is for the gentle, meek, and mild. He waits for us, with grateful hearts, to open our hand and ask for what we desire. The closer you are to Him, the gentler you become. And the more He longs to be generous to you.

> You do not have because
> you do not ask.
> JAMES 4:2

You may have seen videos on the internet where people cause explosions due to careless fireworks. You've probably heard stories of divers swimming with sharks and wishing they hadn't. People get braver and braver with dangerous things if they haven't experienced the danger firsthand.

A healthy respect is important to have when you're in the presence of power of any sort. And of course, the Lord is the most supreme Source of power there is. Fearing God is not a matter of being afraid of Him. It's a matter of standing in great awe, understanding that He is far beyond comprehension, and recognizing that He and His power cannot be harnessed.

Stand in awe of God, and you will be walking in the most rudimentary form of wisdom.

The fear of the LORD is the beginning of wisdom, and the knowledge of the Holy One is understanding.

PROVERBS 9:10

Have you ever had one of those days when a chain of things goes wrong for no apparent reason? Sometimes things just happen that way. Other times, you may sense that you're under attack. And that is very possible.

The spiritual forces of this world are hard at battle. One would undermine God's plan. The other would protect it.

The next time you feel like you're under attack, pray. Tell God your suspicions, and then say what the truth is. You are a child of God, who can't be harmed by the enemy. You can take back your territory and stand victorious every time.

For our struggle is not against flesh and blood,
but against the rulers, against the powers,
against the world forces of this darkness,
against the spiritual forces of wickedness
in the heavenly places.
EPHESIANS 6:12

Worship is more than songs on a Sunday morning. Worship is a lifestyle, meant to be lived by every single believer—whether or not they can sing!

Worship is a response to His holiness. And in order to be able to respond to something, a person needs to experience it. First, we seek, observe, and immerse ourselves in His truth. That can be at church or in the Word, in the forest or on a mountain, or in a conversation with your 16-year-old. Once we experience His presence, it moves us. And we worship Him.

Don't wait for a Sunday morning to "sing praise and worship." Seek out His holiness in life now. Like, *right now*. And respond as you are led.

But an hour is coming, and now is,
when the true worshipers will worship
the Father in spirit and truth; for such people
the Father seeks to be His worshipers.

JOHN 4:23

At this point we understand God's power in limited ways. But there will be a day when not a soul on earth is in ignorance.

The Lord wants His kids with Him. And He wants every person to be His kid. So He waits. But one day soon, things will change.

Already we see His power in oceans and earthquakes, or in the way the sun rises and sets every single day.

Ask Him today if there is just one person who needs just one seed planted in their heart about Jesus. Then be bold to plant it. It could be the very thing that saves them from the day of trouble.

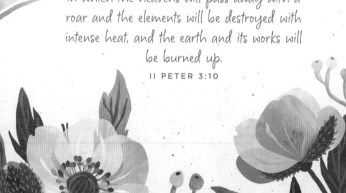

But the day of the Lord will come like a thief, in which the heavens will pass away with a roar and the elements will be destroyed with intense heat, and the earth and its works will be burned up.

II PETER 3:10

"I want to go to the trampoline park! When can we go??"

"As soon as you finish your chores."

"But I want to go *now*!"

"Well, the sooner you finish, the sooner you can go!"

This isn't *quite* how God works. But just imagine. How we live now—and our willingness to bring others to Christ—can actually speed up the process of His coming back. Because God is waiting that no one should perish. But there are those who don't know about Him. That's our job! And the sooner we share His love, the sooner He can come back in full glory. So go shine your light! It *will* make a difference.

Since all these things are to be destroyed in this way, what sort of people ought you to be in holy conduct and godliness, looking for and hastening the coming of the day of God.

II PETER 3:11-12

One dark night, flames exploded across the blackness. The home was gone before the firemen could reach it near the edge of town. To the family, all was lost. At first.

Then the rebuild started. And the new home became a work of love, built by hand by the husband and wife. Insurance money covered the cost of new materials, and all the small details they had hoped for could be added. The new home—pristine and stunning—became a community favorite as the family opened it for ministry and hospitality. Such a thing could never have been imagined before the fire.

We have no idea what new heaven and earth await us after the end. But we can be sure it will blow our socks off.

But according to His promise we are looking for new heavens and a new earth, in which righteousness dwells.

II PETER 3:13

Gideon started with 20,000 soldiers. God whittled it down to 300...and then led the tiny army to victory.

Joshua and Caleb were being taunted by enemy soldiers on a hill. They climbed the hill, an uphill battle...but singlehandedly won it.

Sarai was to birth a nation. She waited 99 years... and then had her firstborn son.

Sometimes God's strategies seem backwards. The thing that makes the very least sense is the very right answer. That's why it's so important to learn to hear His voice. Doing the logical thing isn't always the way He wants us to go.

But when Jesus heard this, He said, "This sickness is not to end in death, but for the glory of God, so that the Son of God may be glorified by it." Now Jesus loved Martha and her sister and Lazarus. So when He heard that he was sick, He then stayed two days longer in the place where He was.

JOHN 11:4-6

He knew it was dangerous. Lethal, even. But he just had this feeling it was his calling. So the missionary doctor turned away from all of the desperate pleas and advice from home, and walked right into the diseased masses. Anyone who got near the patients would be expected to contract the disease—with a 24 hour death timeline—within two days. But he had the Holy Spirit with him, and he believed.

Years later, the doctor spoke of his experience. "I'm not a hero. I'm very weak. But in my weakness He is strong, and that strengthens me."

We're not all anointed against communicable diseases. But you *do* have a special calling on your life. How has God gifted you to uniquely serve others?

The Lord is my helper, I will not be afraid.
What will man do to me?

HEBREWS 13:6

Every person, place and thing were created by God, for His glory. This can sure seem confusing when we see how some things are used against Him! There are musicians with intense talent, singing about all sorts of ungodly things. People with a gift for hearing from the spiritual world, if they don't aim to glorify Him, may end up communicating with evil.

The beauty, and the unpredictable, of free will is that every being gets the choice of how to live. God doesn't want robots. He wants those who love Him to use their gifts for His glory. That means you get to decide—but the benefits of serving Him far outweigh doing things on your own.

For by Him all things were created, both in the heavens and on earth, visible and invisible, whether thrones or dominions or rulers or authorities—all things have been created through Him and for Him.

COLOSSIANS 1:16

Even though all things were created by God and for God, there is only one true God. You can put full confidence in this. No sense in dividing loyalties.

Some people believe in superstitions. Having superstitions is nothing more than placing trust in something other than the *one true God*. Healing stones can't do what the Healer Himself can. Saint is the title given to every one of God's chosen people. And nothing will come of breaking a mirror—unless you accidentally get cut!

All you need is God. His presence. His love. His power. His truth. His hope. His deliverance. His salvation.

Know therefore today, and take it to your heart, that the LORD, He is God in heaven above and on the earth below; there is no other.

DEUTERONOMY 4:39

Princess movies are getting a bad rep these days. They can be seen as chauvinistic and unbalanced: the helpless maiden, trapped in a tower, needing rescue from the brave warrior prince.

But deep inside, we all need rescue. The tender, vulnerable part of us is crying out for hope and help. Movies and stories often reflect this because they reflect the deepest, loneliest parts of our hearts. We need our Savior!

No matter how macho and masculine or tough you are, there's a tenderhearted princess inside wanting a hero. This is nothing to be ashamed of. In fact, it is one of the sweetest gifts from God.

The LORD also thundered in the heavens, and the Most High uttered His voice, hailstones and coals of fire. He sent out His arrows, and scattered them, and lightning flashes in abundance, and routed them...He brought me forth also into a broad place; He rescued me, because He delighted in me.

PSALM 18:13-14, 19

The Hebrew character *he* is depicted by the letter h. This character signifies the breath of life. When the Lord changed Abram's name to Abraham, He was symbolically breathing new life and new purpose into the father of many nations.

And what do we do the moment we are born? Take our first breath.

And what do we do the moment we die? We take our last.

The breath of God is the lifeblood of our bodies. We live because He is constantly giving us breath.

As long as you have breath, praise the Lord. It's because of this breath you *can* praise Him.

The God who made the world and all things in it, since He is Lord of heaven and earth, does not dwell in temples made with hands; nor is He served by human hands, as though He needed anything, since He Himself gives to all people life and breath and all things.

ACTS 17:24, 25

Suspiciously familiar sounds are heard from behind the bedroom door. You check the clock and think the timing is just about right...so you peer in. You see that adorable little form standing up in his crib. His face is turned toward the door, expectant. And the moment he sees your face, he squeals in delight. *"Mama!"* He beams.

If we let Him love us with a Father's love, God can be that source of delight to our days. Certainly, He waits for us to wake up each day. And our delight in Him is His pleasure. Tomorrow morning when you roll over, try saying good morning to God. Wait for His response, and see what kind of effect He has on your day.

*O satisfy us in the morning with
Your lovingkindness, that we may sing for joy
and be glad all our days.*

PSALM 90:14

Hold a tiny acorn. Turn it over in your hand. Look for evidence of...anything? It looks so harmless. Squirrel food, you think.

Now look up at the oak tree the acorn fell from. Seventy feet tall, shaking with strength in the wind. It houses the squirrels who eat its food. It shelters animals and people. Its wood can be used to make some of the strongest furniture you can buy. But where did it come from?

That incredible power, or the potential for it, lives inside one tiny acorn. It doesn't take two or three acorns; just one.

The Holy Spirit lives in you. It doesn't take more than one person; just you. To do the impossible. To serve with power. To stand strong in the midst of storms.

You are from God, little children, and have overcome them; because greater is He who is in you than he who is in the world.

1 JOHN 4:4

There is a fable about a lion and a mouse. The lion has a thorn in his paw, and the tiny mouse—who seemed so helpless a moment before—was able to remove the terrible thorn to make the lion well.

We are less than mice before God. But God loves to use us as partners in His kingdom business. He creates roles for us to play, and listens when we speak. He lets us try out our ideas. The God of the universe—the Lion of Judah—allows us to *help* Him in His work!

You may feel too weak. *Yes, you are!* But His power is all you need to do miraculous things.

Now Mount Sinai was all in smoke because the LORD descended upon it in fire; and its smoke ascended like the smoke of a furnace, and the whole mountain quaked violently. When the sound of the trumpet grew louder and louder, Moses spoke and God answered him with thunder.

EXODUS 19:18-19

One of the great and inexplicable things about the Lord is His omnipresence. That's a big word which simply means God is everywhere! That means He can sit on His throne, the heavens His footstool...and also live confined and infinitely powerful inside each of His children. Likewise, we are spiritual beings in earthly bodies. But we are seated in heavenly places with Christ. This is a powerful tool we can use here and now. The spiritual world is at our fingertips, through the Holy Spirit. This is why prayer and connection with the Lord are so important—to help us see past the present and earthly reality, toward the truth of heaven.

For thus says the high and exalted One Who lives forever, whose name is Holy, "I dwell on a high and holy place, and also with the contrite and lowly of spirit in order to revive the spirit of the lowly and to revive the heart of the contrite."

ISAIAH 57:15

Indiana Jones needed to cross the 50-foot wide chasm. He saw no way. But he had a clue: Only in the lead from the lion's head...

And so on faith, Indiana stuck his foot out. Shakily he stepped forward into nothingness...and landed on a beam. A strong beam. A previously invisible one, which carried him across to the other side.

We may not always *see* the power around us, but that doesn't mean it isn't there. The Lord often reveals His plan at the very moment we *need to see it or else.*

And this is faith. To believe that God is who He says He is. And believing is acting on what you know to be true, whether you see it or not.

The LORD of hosts is with us;
the God of Jacob is our stronghold. Selah.

PSALM 46:11

"The project deadline has just been cut from four months to one week. And if you don't complete it on time, the entire company will miss its deadline and lose thousands of potential dollars. *Can you do it?*"

Because you believe in the power of partnership with Jesus, you say yes. And a miracle unfolds. People chip in. The project gets done. The customer is happy. But more importantly, you've seen God at work in a way you will never forget.

Pay close attention to the impossible opportunities that cross your path. They may be the perfect time to say no. And they may be just the way God wants to show up and amaze you.

For nothing will be impossible with God.

LUKE 1:37

Your checkbook had a great big red number on the balance line. No way to pay it back; the debt was just too big. And you couldn't help it. Just the luck of the draw.

And then came the billionaire with the ridiculous proposition. *I already paid it all. I gave you a fresh start and a full bank account to access at any time.*

Now the choice is up to you. Do you withdraw from that account? Or are you so skeptical that you don't even go to the bank to see if what the billionaire said is true?

Jesus has done the paying. We get to receive, if we're willing. And we get to share the awesome news of debts paid off to anyone who will listen.

For the wages of sin is death,
but the free gift of God is eternal life
in Christ Jesus our Lord.

ROMANS 6:23

There's no trickery in God. He's not the kind of leader who says one thing and does another. He always honors a pure heart. He rewards the faithful, and shows His kindness to generation after generation. You'll never have to worry about being deceived or rejected. Nothing you've done will scare the Lord off or cause Him to punish you. God loves you as you are, blemishes and all.

He looks at the aim of your life and judges based on that. Are you aiming toward Jesus? Success! Are you off base? He'll nudge you right. Are you lost? He'll come find you. His goodness is incomparable.

The LORD is good to those who wait for Him, to the person who seeks Him.

LAMENTATIONS 3:25

Sharing the good news of Jesus is very important. But another huge part of being a member of the body of Christ is to pray for, encourage, and love our fellow believers. We all need it! The world tears down. Love builds up. Hatred sows discord, and prayer strengthens. The Holy Spirit knits us together as two or more of us gather in His name.

Jesus prayed for you and me, and He still intercedes for us. What's your routine? Some people keep a weekly prayer calendar. Others pray for whoever comes to mind. Ask the Lord for a strategy to regularly lift up and love on your Christian community, and you'll *all* be better for it.

I ask on their behalf; I do not ask on behalf of the world, but of those whom You have given Me; for they are Yours; and all things that are Mine are Yours, and Yours are Mine; and I have been glorified in them.

JOHN 17:9-10

This world would be nowhere without Jesus. Think about it: the first time around, it was a flood! God promised He would never destroy the people of the earth again after that. So instead, to solve the brokenness issue, He made a way. And that way was Jesus.

Jesus is the way to God. He is the absolute truth. He is life to all who believe. He is our doorway into heaven.

If there were no Jesus, there would be no existence at this point. Whether the world believes it or not doesn't change the truth. We all desperately need Jesus.

For from Him and through Him and to Him are all things. To Him be the glory forever. Amen.

ROMANS 11:36

They had reached the bottom of the barrel. All that was left in the cupboard were spices, and the fridge contained a half empty jar of pickles. And so they prayed. "We believe You, Lord. We will eat dinner tonight!" And they went about their day with trust in their hearts.

He went off to work at the church, and she began working in the garden. Hours later as she walked around to the front of the house, she noticed bags on the front stoop. Someone had delivered a week's worth of groceries.

The Lord always delivers on His promises. We don't always know when or how, but we can believe. His eye is always on His beloved children.

For this reason I say to you, do not be worried about your life, as to what you will eat or what you will drink; nor for your body, as to what you will put on. Is not life more than food, and the body more than clothing?

MATTHEW 6:25

When in doubt, love it out. That was her motto as she worked at the children's camp for cancer patients. Those kids were often so starving for love and attention. Their bodies, families, and lives had been through so much. They just needed love.

Sometimes she wondered if she cared *too* much. Was that even possible, to over-love? Could she give those children too much kindness and energy?

One day she confided in a wise friend. "Well," the friend responded, "answer me this. Can you imagine reaching heaven, and having Jesus tell you that you loved *too* much? Or might it be more likely that He would say you loved too little? Which would you want to hear?"

From that point she knew. Love is an endless commodity that is worth giving and giving away.

Fight the good fight of faith;
take hold of the eternal life to which you
were called, and you made the good confession
in the presence of many witnesses.

I TIMOTHY 6:12

Husband gets a speeding ticket. *Thank You, Lord, for reminding us to stay safe.* Coffee shop is out of that one drink you count on every day. *Thank You for reminding me what I can live without.* Daughter gets her first C and comes home in tears. *Thank You for challenging us to work through difficult circumstances.*

Everything we face has kingdom value. It can all be cashed in for treasure. And it's often the things that seem least special and wonderful, which have the greatest impact.

The next time you are inconvenienced in some way, try being deliberate to give thanks. It may just change your outlook and make you feel richer in Christ.

Rejoice always; pray without ceasing;
in everything give thanks; for this is God's will
for you in Christ Jesus.
I THESSALONIANS 5:16-18

There's no mountain too high that the Lord can't see over it. No ocean too deep that He can't cross it to reach you. No desert too dry that He can't rain down His love and mercy.

God will stop at nothing to love you. He spares no expense for His children. We can slow Him down with our disbelief, or miss His tenderness if we keep our hearts hard.

But stay soft and pliable, trust Him with your needs, and He'll surprise you. God has all power at His fingertips. But it's you He wants above all else.

Thus says God the LORD, who created
the heavens and stretched them out,
who spread out the earth and its offspring,
who gives breath to the people on it and spirit
to those who walk in it, "I am the LORD."

ISAIAH 42:5-6

It's one of the strangest, most wonderful phenomena in life: loving. Love is made for giving. Hang onto what you have without sharing, and it will grow stagnant in you. You might begin to feel lonely, detached, unloved yourself. But give the love you have—and instead of feeling empty, you'll be filled right back up by the Lord.

He's just waiting for you to share it. You were made for it. And He loves filling your tank as soon as you have room!

God *is* love. So if you have God, you have an endless supply. The more generous you are with it, the more generous He will be with you!

Beloved, let us love one another,
for love is from God; and everyone who loves
is born of God and knows God.

I JOHN 4:7-8

There was a popular game show in the 1980's called *Name That Tune*. Contestants would be given a single clue about the title of a song. Then they would decide how many notes of the song they needed to hear before they guessed the title. It would go something like this: "I can name that song in three notes!"

It was fine to say it. But then the contestant had to listen to the notes and then take a guess. They either got it right or they did not. Winning wasn't based on what they *said* they could do, but on what they could *actually* do.

Evidence speaks volumes, and faith is strengthened on it. Seeing miracles helps a person believe. Experiencing God's love and compassion through others makes all the difference.

Jesus answered and said to them, "Go and report to John what you hear and see: the BLIND RECEIVE SIGHT and the lame walk, the lepers are cleansed and the deaf hear, the dead are raised up, and the POOR HAVE THE GOSPEL PREACHED TO THEM."

MATTHEW 11:4-5

Imagine if your child were being accused of plagiarism in college. The professor and principal are prepared to suspend her based on circumstantial evidence. But you know that she worked all weekend to write the report in her own words! How easy would it be for you to stay quiet when injustice is being served?

We want justice, because our God is a just God. We've been wired to want what is right for ourselves and the ones we love. There's nothing wrong with that! But sometimes the very best policy is to stand back and watch the Lord work, instead of getting angry. He has a plan. And not always, but *sometimes*—we get in the way of what He wants to do.

(He)emptied Himself, taking the form of a bond-servant, and being made in the likeness of men. Being found in appearance as a man, He humbled Himself by becoming obedient to the point of death, even death on a cross.

PHILIPPIANS 2:7-8

For some Christians it's hard to think of being rewarded. After all, we're supposed to be humble and lowly, wanting nothing, not wishing for anything more than what God gives us—right?

But then there's Jesus who, *for the joy set before Him*, endured the cross. He sacrificed for the sake of joy! And what is His joy? You and me! Jesus' example is that the kingdom is full of reward. There's no shame—in fact, there is joy!—in wanting what the Lord has promised. So look forward to all God has for you. It's more than you could dare to think or imagine.

Convinced of this, I know that I will remain and continue with you all for your progress and joy in the faith, so that your proud confidence in me may abound in Christ Jesus through my coming to you again.

PHILIPPIANS 1:25-26

The judge stared down at the defendant, about to make His ruling. "You have admitted your guilt. I have no choice but to sentence you to life in prison." The defendant's father spoke out from the crowd. "Please, your honor! Let me take my son's place!"

"But you too are guilty of murder, sir. You cannot serve two sentences.

The courtroom door opened and a young man walked in. The judge's own son.

"Father, I know I am innocent. But I want to take this man's place. He is guilty. But I want to set him free."

The judge gasped. He was filled with sorrow and love at his own son's selflessness. "So be it," he said. Young man, you are free to go."

He made Him who knew no sin to be sin
on our behalf, so that we might become
the righteousness of God in Him.

II CORINTHIAN'S 5:21

Choosing your attitude is as deliberate as choosing your outfit. How are you going to go about your day? Will you put on a veil of pessimism and entitlement? Or will you choose to wear kindness and encouragement? Will you hope for the best, or expect the worst?

Just as it takes deliberate effort to put pants and a top on, it takes effort to wear the virtues given us by God. Especially in the face of challenges. But consider it an honor. Like wearing a uniform to a job you love, it's a privilege to have His grace and mercy at our fingertips.

So, as those who have been chosen of God, holy and beloved, put on a heart of compassion, kindness, humility, gentleness and patience...Beyond all these things put on love, which is the perfect bond of unity.

COLOSSIANS 3:12, 14

Sometime take a few minutes to read Genesis chapter 1. Really focus on what is happening. In no other place can we read about that kind of miraculous creation. The Lord took nothing...literally *nothing*... and turned into *something*. Skeptics, atheists, and scientists have come up with other theories: that a ball of gas exploded, turning eventually into all life and creation we see today. So, which is harder to believe? That you are the product of a ball of gas, or the creation of a Master artist? It certainly sounds way better to believe you're a work of art! Because you *are*.

By faith we understand that the worlds
were prepared by the word of God,
so that what is seen was not made
out of things which are visible.

HEBREWS 11:3

There are no perfect words when praying to God, except the ones that are most genuine and sincere. But Jesus did give a clue as to how to pray in power.

a) Our Father is glorious and holy: tell Him!

b) His kingdom is perfect: ask for its influence here on earth and in your circumstances.

c) God knows best: let Him lead.

Prayer is most powerful when you partner with God in the way He suggests. Partnership doesn't necessarily mean reading words on a page. It means using *your* heart, *your* voice, and *your* desire to bring His kingdom here today.

Pray, then, in this way:
"Our Father who is in heaven,
hallowed be Your name.
Your kingdom come. Your will be done,
on earth as it is in heaven."

MATTHEW 6:9-10

*Y*ou, friend, are a smart person. You know many things. You've been given all sorts of knowledge and experience. But even the wisest and oldest among us is a mere blip on the screen of God's eternal plan. He is the Master Architect, with a view to everything. Before time began. For the last 2000+ years, And until a new heaven and a new earth take place.

Don't be offended or hurt if something doesn't make sense. There's A LOT you don't know, along with everyone else! God is working *all things* together for good...and that takes a lot of orchestration. Simply trusting Him and following His lead are the most peaceful, restful ways to go.

Do all things
without grumbling or disputing.
PHILIPPIANS 2:14

The United States ambassador to any other country is not in the habit of spilling our country's secrets. Likewise, there is much she doesn't know about the inner workings of our government. Her job is to represent the USA to those she comes in contact with—with honor and respect.

We get to represent heaven every day. We get to share the good things we know of God, and when we don't know, it's okay to say so. Each of us is on a unique journey of learning and growing with the Lord. It's good to be real about our humility and lack of understanding! It tends to make others more comfortable in their own weakness.

Do not be hasty in word or impulsive in thought to bring up a matter in the presence of God. For God is in heaven and you are on the earth; therefore let your words be few.

ECCLESIASTES 5:2

Many companies hire their leadership from the outside—men with years of experience doing similar work. Sometimes that is of great benefit to the company.

Other times, a leader is born from the bottom. He starts as a mail room delivery boy. He moves to various starting positions, learning all the ins and outs of the company—doing the hard work, the leg work, and finally contributing more and more to the company's success. Those leaders, once they reach the top, have a unique way of communicating with and understanding the employees in their care.

Jesus took the long road to His highest position. He started from the bottom in order to reach the lowliest of us all.

Therefore Pilate said to Him, "So You are a king?" Jesus answered, "You say correctly that I am a king. For this I have been born, and for this I have come into the world, to testify to the truth. Everyone who is of the truth hears My voice."

JOHN 18:37

The stars in the sky can be billions of light years away. Yet their shining is so pure that it can be seen by the human eye. Other debris, asteroids, and satellites float around in space, but we cannot see them. It takes the purest light to shine the brightest.

What debris or dark matter interferes with the light you carry? Ask the Lord to remove it.

And at the same time, be encouraged that the light of Jesus can shine through the dark, even where imperfections exist. You are the perfect vessel for His work, and you make a bright difference in the world around you.

Do all things without grumbling or disputing; so that you will prove yourselves to be blameless and innocent, children of God above reproach in the midst of a crooked and perverse generation, among whom you appear as lights in the world.

PHILIPPIANS 2:14-15

This is your day. Right now. This moment. Whatever year you're reading this. At the time your clock currently reads. You can make a difference right now, for the person you're sitting next to. To the child who eats your cooking. To the girl who scans your groceries. To the stranger who just crossed in front of your car. You have this. very. allotted. second. to have an impact on the world. There's no point in waiting, because what if waiting means missing out on the opportunity to bless and be blessed!

A million such moments pass every day: Your chance to change the world, one tiny little seed at a time.

As for the days of our life,
they contain seventy years,
or if due to strength, eighty years,
yet their pride is but labor and sorrow;
for soon it is gone and we fly away.

PSALM 90:10

"What does it taste like?" she asked her brother. "Um...it's hard to describe? You'll just have to taste it for yourself!"

No one can fully explain what it's like to experience the kingdom of God in a very personal, profound way. But once you do, two things happen. *You get it.* You understand what the hype is all about. And *you can't forget it.* Not ever. Nor do you want to!

Psalm 34:8 isn't lying: *Taste and see that the Lord is good. Oh, the joys of those who take refuge in Him!* The taste of God is amazing. Way beyond anything we could do on our own to alter our state of reality. The kingdom of heaven is real *and* unspeakably good.

So then do not be foolish, but understand what the will of the Lord is. And do not get drunk with wine, for that is dissipation, but be filled with the Spirit.

EPHESIANS 5:17-18

Try this experiment. Go out into public and just smile. A lot. At everyone. At the store, the coffee shop, the gym, on the street. Keep a tally of how many people smile back. It may amaze you!

Cheerfulness is contagious. And when you share cheer in the name of Jesus, He helps! You may find yourself growing more and more cheerful as you share the smiles you have. Because He comes along and fills your tank over and over again.

The Lord loves your willingness to give others what He has given you. And there's *only* good that comes from sharing a smile.

Bright eyes gladden the heart;
good news puts fat on the bones.
PROVERBS 15:30

The young mother and her two toddlers show up at the garage sale. She chooses a few kitchen linens. And as she pays, her daughter picks up a stuffed bunny in a basket near the door. "We can't afford that, sweetie." The child seems to understand, and sets it down.

The homeowner pauses, then reaches down and hands the bunny to the girl. "You can have him, honey! I think he needs you to be his friend!"

Mercy costs very little to give, but is a priceless gift to receive. Watch for ways you can hand that gift to those who don't deserve it. And when you do, you may just find it coming back around to you in unexpected ways.

Blessed are the merciful,
for they shall receive mercy.

MATTHEW 5:7

At the school there was a playground. On the playground was a bench. On the bench sat a boy. And the boy needed a friend. But this wasn't a sad story. Because this bench was the friend bench—a place for kids to go and wait if they wanted to play with someone at recess. And other kids knew to pay attention to the bench. If they saw someone sitting there, they would go and make a new friend.

So the boy didn't sit there for long, before another kid from another class came over and introduced himself. And soon the boy was laughing in a rousing game of tag.

You've got what it takes to be a great friend, just as Jesus is. All you need to do is watch for the chance.

If you greet only your brothers,
what more are you doing than others?
Do not even the Gentiles do the same?

MATTHEW 5:47

The children of God are never alone. Sometimes it can feel lonely. Sometimes having people around becomes very important. But in the end, we have the Lord's presence at all times.

If you have Jesus, you have the Holy Spirit. You carry the kingdom of God with you wherever you go. That means you could be in the middle of a pagan country and still carry His light—which can never be extinguished!

Just try turning on a flashlight in a dark room. Does the darkness dampen the light? Or does the light illuminate the darkness?

You were made to shine, not cower. So go be bright with His love.

The LORD will guard your going out and your coming in from this time forth and forever.

PSALM 121:8

The truth is, Jesus is enough.

He is enough when you don't know what to do. He has the answers. Or when you're on the best vacation of your life, it is wonderful—but still less fulfilling than the fullness of Jesus. Measure everything by His standard: total acceptance, absolute joy, complete fulfillment, unending love. What could possibly compare to any of that alone, never mind all together?

Take the joy of Jesus with you, and it will keep the rest of life in perspective. His joy allows you to weather a storm, comfort a friend, and truly enjoy a celebration. When you have Jesus, you have all the confidence in the world to live in joy.

These things I have spoken to you
so that My joy may be in you,
and that your joy may be made full.
JOHN 15:11

Everyday miracles. Are there even such a thing? Can any supernatural occurrence be considered *ordinary*?

But many miracles of Jesus are very subtle. Like the way He brings two people together in love, and knits them together for 50 years or more. Without the Lord, human beings just don't get along that well! Or the way a flower grows. Have you ever studied the perfect symmetry, repeated over and over again in similar colors and sizes. That is no accident!

We become accustomed to the ways that the Lord constantly, consistently provides miracles. But spend any time considering what would not be possible without God, and you'll be in awe again and again.

He said, "The things that are impossible with people are possible with God."

LUKE 18:27

Certain aquatic plants have an organ called a *holdfast*. The holdfast is designed specifically to attach it to a secure foundation. As the water swirls and sea animals brush past, these plants stay rooted in place.

We too have a holdfast of sorts, and it is our faith. When trouble comes, we stay rooted in the Rock of the Lord. When others brush past, we can be firm in our standing.

And with our holdfast faith, we are free to raise our arms. Our feet of faith stay firmly in place, and we can dance undignified before God—like seaweed in the current.

> You are to cling to the LORD your God,
> as you have done to this day.
>
> JOSHUA 23:8

The cross wasn't just a single-purpose salvation. Jesus is a one-stop source of all freedom, joy, and healing. He spared no expense, and thought of everything. Absolutely nothing can be applied as a "yes, but…" or an "everything else except…."

You are covered. You are free. No sin was too much for Jesus, and nothing that ever happened to you that wasn't enveloped by His grace and love. Even now, you are not beyond His saving grace. "I'm a horrible person" is a lie that needs to die in your heart right now. You are not perfect, nor were you meant to be. You are a beautiful, growing, maturing child of God.

He was pierced through for our transgressions,
He was crushed for our iniquities;
the chastening for our well-being fell upon
Him, and by His scourging we are healed.

ISAIAH 53:5

Jesus has a track record for enlisting the least prepared, least expected people. Not because He's a bad judge of character, but because He's the best! He sees potential, adds the necessary training, and transforms the weak into ministers of His grace.

And it doesn't stop after boot camp! Jesus is into continuing education. He remains a mentor for life, leading His people through Holy Spirit courses on love, joy, peace, patience, kindness, goodness, faithfulness, gentleness, and self-control. It's a comprehensive program, designed to bring you to completion with Him one day. So if you're a student, you're in the very best hands. Take courage that Jesus believes in you!

Now as they observed the confidence of Peter and John and understood that they were uneducated and untrained men, they were amazed, and began to recognize them as having been with Jesus.

ACTS 4:13

What's done is done. The past is past. If it was good, relish in the completion of it. If it was bad, be thankful that the blood of Jesus covers all. But there's just way too much *now* to spend time worrying about *then*. Focus on what is going on around you and how you fit into it all. There's so much opportunity within your current reach, and you don't want to miss it!

The beautiful thing is, the more you dwell in the present with the Lord, the more it sets you up for the future He has planned for you. So the only tense you need to focus on today is the present.

Jesus said to him, "No one, after putting his hand to the plow and looking back, is fit for the kingdom of God."

LUKE 9:62

Baby gorillas spend the first two to three years living on their mother's back. Where mom goes, baby goes. Whatever adventure she embarks on, the mother takes her baby with her. Even if it's dangerous. But the baby finds security in his mother's warm fur and muscled back. He doesn't yet need to fight off predators or dangers, because he is protected.

The Lord remains our shield and protector throughout our lives. We can be strong by proxy— we're riding along on the back of our powerful Father. Nothing should shake us in His presence!

On the flip side, leaving His presence is a dangerous choice. So stay close and enjoy the security of His arms.

Finally, be strong in the Lord and in the strength of His might.

EPHESIANS 6:10

She looks down at her tight-laced skates, takes a deep breath, and steps out onto the rink. *Whoops!* Slippery! This is going to be an adventure! She wobbles along, holding tight to the wall for a while. She is thankful for knee and elbow pads.

As she starts to go down for yet another tumble, she feels a hand reach under her arm. *Daddy!* He holds her up, then grabs her hand tightly. Together they skate along—he on steady feet, and she on wobbly legs. But her confidence is already soaring in his firm grip.

If you stay connected to God, He will not let your foot slip. It takes two to hold hands...so if you grip Him, He promises to grip you back.

Now to Him who is able to keep you from stumbling, and to make you stand in the presence of His glory blameless with great joy, to the only God our Savior, through Jesus Christ our Lord, be glory, majesty, dominion and authority, before all time and now and forever. Amen.

JUDE 24, 25

The word "idol" seems foreign, like ancient history. But the enemy works his subtle ways to bring empty things into our line of worship. Anything you need to check with before making a decision just may be an idol to you! A smoker anxiously thinks about her next opportunity for a cigarette when she travels. A man gets very angry with his wife for accidentally deleting his recording of the game he missed. Inappropriate emotion regarding an object or source of focus may just be a sign that something other than the Lord has your attention. Don't fret—just check in with God. He'll set your feet on the right path.

For they exchanged the truth of God for a lie, and worshiped and served the creature rather than the Creator, who is blessed forever. Amen.

ROMANS 1:25

The shell went off near the soldier's feet, and he is bleeding badly. Gunfire and shouts are everywhere. He cannot move on his own. He begins to panic. Hopelessness sets in.

Suddenly his battalion commander comes into view. He reaches down to grab the wounded man's shoulder. "Let me clear a path, and I'll come back for you. *I promise.*"

Years later, the once wounded man spoke at a veteran's event. "The war around me didn't change, but the peace did for me in that moment because I chose to trust my commander. He said he would come back, and he did."

Jesus has promised to come back for you, and you can carry His peace in knowing He always keeps His word.

If I go and prepare a place for you,
I will come again and receive you to Myself,
that where I am, there you may be also.

JOHN 14:3

No one was meant to do this thing alone. And the most successful believers are often the ones who have learned to strengthen themselves in the Lord. It's good to have friends who can encourage you and speak truth. But the most readily available source of reminders and comfort, along with the Holy Spirit, is His Word.

The God-breathed Bible is a tangible and Spirit-filled place to go when you need to learn, or be reminded of, what is true. The world can be confusing and distracting. People without the anchor of Jesus are not a good source of wisdom or example. But the Word sets your feet on a firm foundation and sets your mind on things above.

> I wait for the LORD, my soul does wait,
> and in His word do I hope.

PSALM 130:5

Emotions are a gift from the Lord! Even Jesus wept with sorrow, felt anger, and sang in happiness. Emotions are a great signal for what's going on inside of you, and should be paid attention to.

Emotions are always most effective when they are surrendered and submitted to God. After all, as the Creator of both our emotions and our means of feeling and expressing them, He knows best what to do with them! Allow Him to lead you through your emotions, and at the right times you will be able to respond in love and confidence to others. Allow your emotions to control you, and you may find yourself saying or doing things you regret later.

A gentle answer turns away wrath,
but a harsh word stirs up anger.

PROVERBS 15:1

Sparks drifted lazily through the smoke as dry wood crackled. The cave had warmed nicely, and the hikers enjoyed full bellies from the trout they had caught earlier in the day and just roasted. They drowsily watched the flames and told stories.

Outside was a different scene. The wind blew almost sideways, and heavy raindrops pelted the side of the steep rocks around the cave. But deep in the cavernous space with their campfire, the hikers were happy.

From under the shelter of the Lord, we can go anywhere and do anything. His covering allows us to live free and confident. Do not be afraid of what rages around you, when you stay close and tucked in with God.

He who dwells in the shelter of the Most High will abide in the shadow of the Almighty. I will say to the LORD, "My refuge and my fortress, My God, in whom I trust!"

PSALM 91:1-2

There's nothing magical about being baptized. In fact, baptism is not even a necessary act in order to be saved by Jesus. But baptism is a demonstration of your acceptance of the gift of salvation.

As you slide under the water it represents death. You must hold your breath under water, so the breath of life stops for just a moment. As the person baptizing you lifts you up, it signifies new life! When you were saved, you traded the old man of sin for the new life of a Saint in the kingdom!

Baptism is for you—a symbolic act. And an act of demonstration for the world. That what Christ has done for you is real, wonderful...and worth dying for in order to live again.

Therefore we have been buried with Him through baptism into death, so that as Christ was raised from the dead through the glory of the Father, so we too might walk in newness of life.

ROMANS 6:4

All the animals in all the world gather in a meeting. The king of the animals (a lion?) says, "Here's the deal. We're each going to take part of the world to live in and call our own. The very best land goes up for auction first. Who wants it? Immediately the gorillas, hippos, and elephants step forward. They're all ready to fight.

But the king speaks up. "Hold up, fellas. I know you can hold your own, and even fight to win what you want. But I'm going to intervene. You, sheep. You could never win a battle for the best prize. So this very good land is for you, no strings attached."

That's the grace of the kingdom. You could never earn what God has for you...but it is yours.

Do not be afraid, little flock,
for your Father has chosen gladly
to give you the kingdom.
LUKE 12:32

Before a child learns to temper her imagination, she can think up impossible storylines with the least likely adventures, with the most amazing gusto. Where else are you likely to hear of the purple penguin who befriends a spotted buffalo as they search for rainbow tokens worth special candy prizes in the lightning bug forest?

But even as wild as a child's imagination can be, the plans of God are even more unfathomable. We see dim glimpses through the Word: seas of glass, streets of gold, angels like many-eyed beings...but God's dreams and plans for us will never be seen this side of heaven. So for now, dream huge. Keep dreaming. And watch as He overwhelms you with even more.

Now to Him who is able to do far more
abundantly beyond all that we ask or think,
according to the power that works within us,
to Him be the glory.

EPHESIANS 3:20-21

It has been said that pride is a two-sided coin. On one side a person says, I am better than you. On the other side, a person says, I am just dirt and dust in order to gain sympathy and attention.

False humility is a trap, but humility is a virtue. The more we, as vessels of God, can decrease and let Him shine through...the more striking and influential we become.

Never be afraid to shine. But hide yourself in the Lord first. That way, you'll know that what shines through you is a true glimpse of heaven.

Let your light shine before men in such a way
that they may see your good works,
and glorify your Father who is in heaven.

MATTHEW 5:16

There was a popular television show in recent years called Person of Interest. A man named Mr. Reese learns the names of individuals who are about to be in grave danger. Until the danger presents itself, it is Mr. Reese's job to secretly follow the individual around the city. He inevitably appears at just the right moment to save the person from the hands of those who mean harm.

The Lord has legions of angels at His fingertips, and as His child, you are the subject of His great care and concern. Call on Him to guard you, and you may just benefit from the armies of angelic forces who are on His side.

For He will give His angels charge concerning you, to guard you in all your ways.

PSALM 91:11

There will come a day when comparison is a thing of the past. No more "keeping up with the Joneses." No more competition between neighbors and friends—unless it's just a fun game of ping pong (if that exists in heaven)! Girls won't feel pressured to dress in the latest fashions. Boys won't try to show off with their latest skateboarding tricks. Or if they do, the oohs and ahhs of the crowd will be genuinely impressed!

The kingdom of heaven is full of those who rejoice with those who rejoice. Practicing it then will be an everyday occurrence. Practicing it now will make you a hot commodity!

We are your reason to be proud as you also are ours, in the day of our Lord Jesus.

II CORINTHIANS 1:14

our friend shows up to lunch after a vacation overseas. You notice she has a fancy new handbag. "I got it for such an incredible price, only twenty dollars! It would cost two hundred here!" As you admire the bag, you glance again at the name brand. You squint...and see that the famous label is misspelled. You've spotted an impostor.

The true things of God don't have to try and convince anyone of their goodness. The closer you scrutinize, the more integrity you see in His handiwork. Not so with impostors, who have to hide blemishes. The Lord doesn't mind close examination. In fact, He welcomes it.

Beware of the false prophets, who come to you in sheep's clothing, but inwardly are ravenous wolves. You will know them by their fruits.

MATTHEW 7:15, 16

What had happened between them was years ago, but it had formed a deep rift between the once-friends. For years the two of them struggled to serve together in their ministry. But things finally crumbled beyond repair...at least beyond repair by the world's standards.

Instead of giving up, the women met a year after they had separated. They opened up about the hard things, shed a few tears, and showed one another the grace God had given them. They tried again. And this time, they experienced the restoration of the Spirit.

Every effort means never giving up on the people in your life. Even if it takes years and is full of mistakes. Leaving room for the Holy Spirit to do amazing things is always rarely wasted time.

With all humility and gentleness, with patience, showing tolerance for one another in love, being diligent to preserve the unity of the Spirit in the bond of peace.

EPHESIANS 4:2-3

It was black. A no moon night, and the teens hadn't planned ahead well enough to get back to camp before dark. They were in a strange forest, with a path that was difficult to spot in daylight, never mind darkness!

One boy had a tiny flashlight on his keychain. So the teens all grabbed hands in a long line. The flashlight-boy led, and in utter blindness, the rest of the campers followed by feel alone.

Learning to hear and understand can be challenging enough in this world! But without God's Word, the way is dark. Sometimes the truth of God is just enough light to see the next step. Other times, it illuminates entire pathways. Either way, trusting His Word is the only way to walk with vision.

Your word is a lamp to my feet
and a light to my path.
PSALM 119:105

There is literally nothing beyond God's control! And there's literally nothing the two of you can't accomplish together. Even when the need is huge and impossible. Your earnest prayers can yield groundbreaking, news-making results.

A wise man once said, when God wants to perform a miracle, He creates an impossible situation. And you, who know the God of the universe on a first Name basis, understand His power. So you aren't intimidated by "impossible." You are hopeful. Excited, even, if you've seen Him work before.

The next time you're tempted to cower in defeat, rise up! And see what God will do.

Elijah was a man with a nature like ours, and he prayed earnestly that it would not rain, and it did not rain on the earth for three years and six months. Then he prayed again, and the sky poured rain and the earth produced its fruit.

JAMES 5:17-18

When you become a parent, it doesn't take long to learn that what you do and say are being watched. You soon encounter adorable moments where a toddler repeats "oh goodness!" or "okie doke," or whatever you're apt to say in everyday life. You also learn quickly, if you have a tendency to say or do things that are not appropriate for a two year old!

Children are wired to mimic and learn from the world around them. As children of God, so are we. That's why it's so important to look to the Lord for our example. If not, our default will be to learn from the world.

Who is watching you today? And where do you have your own eyes trained?

We love, because He first loved us.

I JOHN 4:19

Isn't it just like us to assume God isn't paying attention? We aren't comfortable, we feel insecure, so we assume that God isn't holding up His end of the bargain.

But what if He is the perfect example of how we should carry ourselves through the storm? What if, instead of assuming He's got it wrong, we trust He's got it very right? What if our default is to look to Him and mimic His movements? Chances are, we would experience a much more peaceful existence. And instead of being shaken by whatever comes our way, we would likely be the ones doing the shaking.

And there arose a fierce gale of wind, and the waves were breaking over the boat so much that the boat was already filling up. Jesus Himself was in the stern, asleep on the cushion; and they woke Him and said to Him, "Teacher, do You not care that we are perishing?"

MARK 4:37-38

Have you ever watched an illusionist perform the trick where he says he will cut a woman in half? Although you know it must be an illusion, isn't there just a twinge of fear or disgust as you watch the sword being inserted all the way through the box where her torso appears to be?

We can be skeptics in the face of things we don't understand. At times it is justified—we don't expect a woman to die before an audience being entertained! At other times, especially when God moves, it is best to stand in awe and simply file His work under "Things I Won't Understand Until Heaven." But instead of being terrified of His power or doubting it, believe God is even more amazing than you can comprehend.

And He got up and rebuked the wind and said to the sea, "Hush, be still." And the wind died down and it became perfectly calm. (The disciples) became very much afraid and said to one another, "Who then is this, that even the wind and the sea obey Him?"

MARK 4:39, 41

If we truly understood the dynamics of God's justice, we would probably stand back and relax even when life was unfair. It is simply by His will and word that the planets remain suspended in space. He could flick His finger, and nations would disappear in a puff of smoke.

And in the end, when the battle is over, the only thing remaining will be His kingdom. The enemy fights now because he still thinks he can win. But Jesus.

Evil, harsh things don't stand a chance. Literally. You have God on your side, and while it's hard for a short season, the only news will be good news when the time is right.

Who understands the power of Your anger and Your fury, according to the fear that is due You?

PSALM 90:11

Have you ever read the Bible? Like, all of the parts? If so, you've encountered some pretty amazing stories. War, murder, adultery, prostitution, betrayal, disobedience, and all sorts of sin. Those who look at the Bible as a rule book for what to do, can become very confused. Sometimes the examples in the Bible are of what not to do! We can learn from both!

The Holy Spirit helps us to discern what is true and right from what is unhealthy and wrong. With Him, we have every resource to walk in hope and freedom. With Him, we learn from the best.

For whatever was written in earlier times was written for our instruction, so that through perseverance and the encouragement of the Scriptures we might have hope.

ROMANS 15:4

The Master sat at His work table, pen in hand, tapping ink tip to the edge of His lips. Let's see, He thought. The world will need a very specific set of gifts from this one. I will place her in this city, where she and her husband will meet. I will start her off in this family—they will be just the right mix for her to grow and prepare. She will enjoy animals very much. And I'll give her the gift of compassion. I will set her in this ministry to fulfill her desire to serve. If she chooses to follow Me, she will live a long and fruitful life of this many days.

He planned you out to the last detail. There's nothing that can change who He dreamed you to be or how you can impact your world.

In Your book were all written the days
that were ordained for me,
when as yet there was not one of them.

PSALM 139:16

The Lord wants people to know Him, because once they do, they will fall in love. And loving God leads to life.

Sometimes that means making things so very obvious that a victory or success came from nowhere but Him.

For you and me, that can be an intimidating situation! It requires great faith to believe He'll come through in the ways we need Him to.

The next time you find yourself in a situation that truly requires a miracle, pay close attention. It may just be the Lord, setting you up to be part of His next great storyline.

The LORD said to Gideon, "The people who are with you are too many for Me to give Midian into their hands, for Israel would become boastful, saying, 'My own power has delivered me'...I will deliver you with the 300 men... so let all the other people go."

JUDGES 7:2, 7

It's never, ever too late to turn back. But one of the most gentlemanly things about God is that He never forces repentance or acceptance of Him. That's our choice, in our timing. But in order to have the fullest relationship and life with Him, it's a choice we do have to make.

When we're ready, He's waiting. On the edge of His seat. Watching for you to appear on the horizon, humbled and hungry. He will run to you, announcing to everyone that His child has returned.

It's not always a complete life turnaround we need, it could be disobedience or a built-up wall in one area of life. But the Lord wants all of you. And He can't wait for you to come!

(If) My people who are called by My name humble themselves and pray and seek My face and turn from their wicked ways, then I will hear from heaven, will forgive their sin and will heal their land.

II CHRONICLES 7:14

Science has a term called hypothesis: or a theory to be tested in order to determine its validity. A hypothesis is often called an "If/then statement." If water is brought to a temperature of 212 degrees farenheit, then it will boil.

The Bible is full of If/then statements too. But instead of theories, God's If/then's are promises. If we ask, He will answer. If we believe, He will do it. If we humble ourselves, He will hear us.

It couldn't be clearer: If we follow His ways, then He will deliver on all of His promises. If we draw near to the Creator of the universe, accepting the truth of Jesus, then we will have eternal life.

If we confess our sins,
He is faithful and righteous
to forgive us our sins
and to cleanse us from all unrighteousness.

I JOHN 1:9

What martial artist do you know who, for his very first tournament, steps into the black belt ring and wins? Nobody! It takes years of dedication and training to excel to the point of champion. And how many Olympic athletes get to the game in the first year of their sport?

Training is an absolute necessity for anyone wanting to succeed. It is the same for every believer. We need knowledge and understanding. Practice succeeding, and practice failing. Direction from God and from trusted friends. We need work!

Train hard with the Word and with the Holy Spirit, and you will have favor in whatever you put your hand to.

All Scripture is inspired by God and profitable for teaching, for reproof, for correction, for training in righteousness; so that the man of God may be adequate, equipped for every good work.

II TIMOTHY 3:16-17

*S*he was a mess, and the town knew it. Married and divorced four times. Living with another man. Not the most reputable neighbor. In fact, she was so shunned that the normal social activity for women in the town was an event she avoided every day. She went by herself to draw water when no one else was around.

When Jesus spoke, He changed her life. And she knew it. And when she, a normally edgy and reserved woman, went running through the streets with excitement, it was clear something had changed!

We will overcome by the blood of the Lamb and the word of our testimony (Rev. 12:11). So tell the world—just start with your neighbors—what God has done in your life. It may just make history.

From that city many
of the Samaritans believed in Him
because of the word of the woman who testified,
"He told me all the things
that I have done."

JOHN 4:39

God dares you. Just try to think of one thing that is too big and bad and ugly for Him to redeem and erase by the blood of Jesus! In the end, you'll only discover that you are truly free, by His standards. Even that little thing yesterday doesn't throw Him for a loop either. He's not mad at you for messing up even though you're supposed to be a "good Christian." He simply asks for your humble heart to turn toward Him, recognize your weakness, and allow Him to start you over.

But the tax collector...
was beating his breast, saying,
"God, be merciful to me, the sinner!"
I tell you, this man went
to his house justified.
LUKE 18:13, 14

The most difficult circumstances are often the most effective ways for the Lord to get through to us. If we're willing to learn, He is willing to walk us through to the other side of maturity and endurance and hope. Those who have been there, know. It's hard to say "I would do that all over again" knowing how you've grown. But the truth is, once you've come out freer and full of deeper joy, you're willing to experience whatever is needed in order to know Him better.

Use your circumstances to strengthen those around you. Talk about the hard of it, and the beauty that most certainly comes from ashes. Ask God to show you what He is doing that you can share.

Now I, Nebuchadnezzar, praise, exalt and honor the King of heaven, for all His works are true and His ways just, and He is able to humble those who walk in pride.

DANIEL 4:37

An ant is intent on one thing: food. Its job throughout the summer is to store up for winter. It works hard. It would probably be fair to say that the ant wouldn't understand the life of a housecat, which has much more to do with sleeping and causing mischief!

If an ant were to consider a housecat, it would have all kinds of criticisms. What a lazy waste of an animal body, it might think.

But to a housecat, who snuggles with a warm owner each night or delights in the sun-warmed chair arm, life would be silly any other way.

God does not fit in a human-box any more than a housecat fits in an ant-box. Let Him show you who He is and what He can do. It will open your eyes to incredible new things.

Great is our Lord and abundant in strength;
His understanding is infinite.

PSALM 147:5

Joseph never expected to end up in prison. But by a strange turn of events there he was, condemned to life in a dungeon due to false accusations. But Joseph was not alone in Spirit, because God was with Him. He was not empty of mind, because He knew the Scriptures and the truth of God's word. And when the time came, Joseph's faith brought Him into favor with his cellmate—and eventually, the nation's leader.

Hide the word in your heart (Psalm 119), and it will definitely benefit you and the world around you. You never know, until you need it, how rich a memory bank full of Scriptural truth can be.

This book of the law shall not depart from your mouth, but you shall meditate on it day and night, so that you may be careful to do according to all that is written in it; for then you will make your way prosperous, and then you will have success.

JOSHUA 1:8

His body shook as he slid into the driver's seat. How much more of this could he take? His wife's postpartum sadness had morphed into full-blown depression. Life at home was miserable.

There was nowhere to turn...except up. And like a tender-hearted child, he wept. He poured His heart out to God, the One he knew had all the answers.

It took a while. But as he sat there shivering in the car, he began to feel a warmth in his soul. The raw brokenness of his heart felt—well—enveloped in the tender love of God. It was as though he were being held.

God is many things. And one is the kindest Father you could ask for, in all the times you need Him most. He can be trusted with every piece of your heart.

Like a shepherd He will tend His flock, in His arm He will gather the lambs and carry them in His bosom; He will gently lead the nursing ewes.

ISAIAH 40:11

You can read all the books. Take all the classes. Watch all the others doing it. But until you find yourself challenged to love the unlovable, such a thing will only be a concept. It's easy to love when the feelings are there. But what about when it's the last thing you feel like doing?

Getting to know Jesus means benefitting from the purest love known to man. And as that experience washes over you, it won't be long before you are so full yourself that loving others will be an act of love to Jesus, your very favorite.

Serving others through a love for Jesus, makes loving the unlovable a whole lot easier—and very rewarding.

If you love Me, you will keep My commandments. He who has My commandments and keeps them is the one who loves Me.

JOHN 14:15, 21

In Snow White and the Seven Dwarfs, one dwarf stands out. He's the one who needs warming over. The one who always calls attention to the negative. The one the others spend time ignoring, until that one moment when his heart goes soft. Grumpy is definitely not the productive one in the group. In fact, most of the time, the other dwarves are productive in spite of him, not because of him.

Feelings, even anger, are natural. But with the grace of God we can learn to respond instead of react. There are many things that merit our anger. But few things are accomplished when we let our anger lead.

For the anger of man does not achieve
the righteousness of God.

JAMES 1:20

Everything hinges on God. This is His world, and we are His creation. When we act apart from that truth, it's like driving around a mail truck without delivering any mail. What's the point?!? And worse is the fact that our mail truck—or our motivations, passions, giftings and energy—are not just wasted when we don't use them. It actually has a negative benefit to the kingdom of God. Because He is counting on us to deliver. We're not just plastic, unimportant extras. He has given us shoes to fill that no one else can.

You are needed. You have something to deliver. People are waiting on you to shine your light, so that they can see the way.

Whatever is not from faith is sin.

ROMANS 14:23

If I give all my possessions to feed the poor, and if I surrender my body to be burned, but do not have love, it profits me nothing.

I CORINTHIANS 13:3

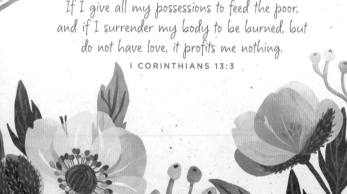

What wouldn't a diehard fan do to sit on the 50 yard line during the Super Bowl? How many chores and how much homework would a young girl do to be allowed to see that band in concert?

Perhaps "fandom" of this world is put into place so that we can experience the true level of what passion for the Lord could look like. Telling everyone what you get to do! Losing your voice for the excitement and screaming! Talking for hours on end to fellow fans!

Of course, head-over-heels love for Jesus looks a bit different because motivations are different. But maybe we can use outside examples to examine our own hearts about our enthusiasm for Christ.

You shall love the LORD your God with all your heart and with all your soul and with all your might.

DEUTERONOMY 6:5

The kingdom of God is such peace. It is not about fighting, so much as it is about releasing the fight to the Lord. It is not about winning, so much as it is about sharing awesome news. It is not about striving, so much as it is about allowing the work of your hands to be a blessing in every way.

His ways are far more attractive than religious views would have you think. There is no earning a place in heaven. Only receiving your adoption. There is no doing in order to be loved, there is only doing because you are loved. It's the most joyful way to walk in this world: Come to Jesus, and you will find rest.

*What does the LORD require of you
but to do justice, to love kindness,
and to walk humbly with your God?*

MICAH 6:8

Several years ago there was a short film called "Validation" circulating around the internet. It featured a young man who took it upon himself to change his parking validation booth into a place for people to receive personal validation. When they reached the front of the line, the young man would compliment and encourage each traveler. Of, course, the line grew to be so long it reached around the block.

People are hungry to be seen, known, and loved for who they are. And it's no mistake that God made us to be encouragers for that very reason. There's never a moment when building one another up with our words and actions is a bad idea!

But encourage one another day after day, as long as it is still called "Today."

HEBREWS 3:13

At a young age, a child learns to squeeze his eyes tight and grasp his hands together at the table when it's time to pray. Most likely, he learns because his parents begin showing him that classic posture of prayer when they want him to learn that praying is important. Most adults don't squeeze their eyes and hands together when they speak with God. Why? Because they know that prayer is deeper than hand motions; it is a heart-to-heart conversation. What we look like when we pray doesn't matter, really.

There's a lot we learn in the beginning that serves to get us started, but we make adjustments as we internalize the true meanings behind our actions. What God cares about is the inside—not the looks.

Whether, then, you eat or drink or whatever you do, do all to the glory of God.

I CORINTHIANS 10:31

In the 1950's Jim Elliot was one of four missionaries who traveled deep into Ecuador to reach the Huaorani tribe for Christ. He knew it was very dangerous. And sure enough, all four of the men were killed by the Huaorani.

But Jim's wife Elisabeth continued his mission. She served the tribe in love, and eventually they saw that what at first seemed very foreign, was a beautiful display of Jesus. The Huaorani eventually accepted Jesus, and they are warriors for Christ to this day.

The things of Jesus are truly foreign in this world. It's supposed to be that way, because we belong to a world that is way, way better.

I have given them Your word; and the world
    has hated them, because they are not of
    the world, even as I am not of the world.

JOHN 17:14

A wise worship leader once said, "Live a lifestyle of repentance." Does that mean constantly beating yourself up, punishing yourself, and recalling all the things you've done wrong lately? Of course not! Repentance is a change of mind, or a 180 degree turn from sin toward God. A lifestyle of repentance involves constantly adjusting course toward God and away from sin. Sin separates us from God. So repentance means breaking down those walls by receiving His forgiveness, and determining to change behavior so that you won't be in that position again. The mercy of God is there for the taking, if you're willing to humbly take your place at His feet.

In repentance and rest you will be saved,
in quietness and trust is your strength.

ISAIAH 30:15

Amen: so be it.

Firmness, stability, constancy. All are qualities we long for in friendship. Spouses. Home life. Job situations and business relationships.

Jesus is all of that and more. Of all the many, many promises made to us by God, every single one of them is fulfilled in Jesus. Can you have perfect peace? Yes. Jesus. Can you release worry and live with undying hope? Jesus. But that one situation, can you really expect to be forgiven for that? Jesus!

By His very life, death, and resurrection, Jesus says "So be it" to every good and perfect gift of God.

For as many as are the promises of God, in Him they are yes; therefore also through Him is our Amen to the glory of God through us.

II CORINTHIANS 1:20

*L*ife with the Holy Spirit is full of the glorious unknown. For some, the idea of keeping things fluid seems very hard! But for those who have learned to enjoy the freedoms of the Spirit, big plans are always subject to His will to interrupt, change, adapt, and improve upon things. Remember, He is the only One who sees the big picture. What may make perfect sense to you, could be in conflict with the overall purpose God has for your family or surroundings. Yes, the goal is to be in communication with Him from the beginning of plan-making. But every moment with the Lord is a chance for relationship growth and learning. Just take it as it comes, and you'll find a peace that passes understanding.

Come now, you who say, "Today or tomorrow we will go to such and such a city, and spend a year there and engage in business and make a profit." Yet you do not know what your life will be like tomorrow.

JAMES 4:13, 14

We can always take God at His word. Even when He says something that seems innocuous or obvious. Honor my parents? Yes, of course I do that. But examine the word honor: To revere; to respect; to treat with deference and submission, and perform relative duties to. What is your parents' and elders' current situation? Are you loving them well, or taking them for granted? Do you place their very best interest and comfort before your own?

When God says that honoring your parents will make things go well for you, you can believe Him. Try adapting your behavior this month, and just see if your own life is blessed by it.

Honor your father and mother...
so that it may be well with you,
and that you may live long on the earth.
EPHESIANS 6:2, 3

It's fair to assume that anything eternal is more valuable than anything temporary. Your relationship with Jesus will be forever. Your relationships with other believers as well. The fruit of the Spirit, all training of perseverance and character, and all kingdom service will remain. Everything else falls to second.

Good sleep, balanced meals, exercise and lots of water serve your ability to walk out the eternal values of this life. But knowing His Word—and more importantly, knowing Him—will train you for things to come. Neither should be neglected. But if you spend more time at the gym than you do in His presence, it may make sense to make some adjustments.

For bodily discipline is only of little profit, but godliness is profitable for all things, since it holds promise for the present life and also for the life to come.

1 TIMOTHY 4:8

They've been married for 46 years. They know each other well—all the qualities and all the quirks. She knows his likes and dislikes. So when she speaks for both of them, she does so with a desire to honor the kind of man he is. She would never, for example, commit him to a dance-off at the local charity event! Likewise, he knows her. He likes to cook. But he would never commit her to cooking for one of his work events. Cooking is not her thing.

Love means caring very much to respect who the other person is. The Lord, in His amazing love, does this for us. And when we love Him well, we are acting on His behalf with that same kind of deference.

Let the words of my mouth and the meditation of my heart be acceptable in Your sight, O LORD, my rock and my Redeemer.

PSALM 19:14

The group of women sat around a craft table, tissue paper and pipe cleaners in hand. One woman had mastered the art of paper flower making. The others were learning. So six pairs of eyes were trained on the one set of skilled hands. They mimicked each movement as those hands bunched and wrapped a colorful flower together.

Jesus is our ultimate goal-reacher. He has been there, right at the beginning where we began. And now He sits victoriously in heaven! He has the joy we long for, and the road He took to get there was brutal. But He succeeded. And we long to as well. So we watch Jesus, knowing His joy and His victory will be ours if we endure the fight.

Fixing our eyes on Jesus, the author and perfecter of faith, who for the joy set before Him endured the cross, despising the shame, and has sat down at the right hand of the throne of God.

HEBREWS 12:2

In springtime, the Siskyou mountain range can be treacherous for truckers traveling between Oregon and California. At that time of year, the top of the pass is still prone to blizzard conditions.

Truckers know that when a blizzard begins, they have two important touch points. Watch for the lights of the vehicle in front of you. And watch for the tracks made by those gone before. If you're the first one through, you become the trailblazer. But you know that for anyone behind you, the path will be safer and better.

The Holy Spirit is our trailblazer through life. Without Him, people are wandering and confused. With Him, it may not be easy—but it will definitely be safer and more sure.

You will make known to me the path of life;
in Your presence is fullness of joy;
in Your right hand there are pleasures forever.

PSALM 16:11

If you've seen the *Hobbit* movies from recent years, chances are you can recall the moment when the hobbit Bilbo steps into the caverns under the Lonely Mountain. For as far as the eye can see, there is gold and priceless treasure. In all his years a single small hobbit could never make use of all that cavern held.

Apply that image, if you can, to the treasure troves of heaven. Mounds of wisdom. Endless supplies of miracles and gifts. You wouldn't even know where to begin, much less spend it all!

That is what we have access to. The Lord is endless, and so rich with treasure. He invites us in. No dangerous dragon guarding the doorway. Just an open invitation to come.

Oh, the depth of the riches both of the wisdom and knowledge of God! How unsearchable are His judgments and unfathomable His ways!

ROMANS 11:33

Radios aren't used much anymore; especially radios with actual dials. But there was a time when finding a clear signal for your chosen radio station involved a steady, delicate touch and a keen ear. Turning the knob just a percentage of a millimeter could affect the static and background noise behind the music.

The voice of the Holy Spirit can be that fine-tuned. He is not hard to hear. But it does take supreme focus, and a desire to actually locate the sound of His voice. It takes a willingness to release all other distractions and listen beyond the static noises of the world. And there, in the stillness, is the most beautiful sound. Truth.

After the wind an earthquake,
but the LORD was not in the earthquake.
After the earthquake a fire, but the LORD
was not in the fire; and after the fire a sound of
a gentle blowing.

I KINGS 19:11, 12

According to the 1828 version of Webster's dictionary, to know means "to have clear and certain perception; not to be doubtful."

Knowing is a verb. Which means, knowing is an action. It is a deliberate act on our behalf to do something.

When the image on the screen shows a baby who hardly moves, and a slow heartbeat, you need to put that verb to use. Know that He is God. Above the visible.

When the divorce is final, and the fact that you're officially single hits you hard...know that He is God. Above the unknown.

It's not your job to understand all the things. But you do have an opportunity to do more than just sit and wait. You can know.

Cease striving and know that I am God.

PSALM 46:10.

Would you rather have a friend who needs the last word, or a friend whose goal is to help you feel heard?

Would you rather talk with someone whose fuse is short, or someone who doesn't even carry matches that would light the fuse?

One of the best ways to be a good friend is to be the kind of friend you yourself would like to have. It takes practice, which means you have to take risks. You have to get out there. Make some mistakes. Find yourself in a sticky situation or conflict, and don't shy away. Instead, determine to be the kind of friend who wants to see things through in love.

> But everyone must be quick to hear,
> slow to speak and slow to anger.
>
> JAMES 1:19

It was her second time behind the wheel—a stick shift, no less—and she kept killing the engine. "Mom, I'll never get this right! I'm a horrible driver!"

"Honey, you are fifteen years old and you are learning. You are at the exact level of driving ability you're supposed to be! You'll get better!"

The end is not the goal for everyday life. The journey is! Where you are today is where God wants you. He's growing you, maturing you, and bringing you to completion over time.

God works at different paces, in different ways, with every person. Focus on your own adventure, and you'll get the most out of it as you go.

For I am confident of this very thing,
that He who began a good work in you
will perfect it until the day of Christ Jesus.

PHILIPPIANS 1:6

"I wish I had a million dollars."

"What have you done about that?"

"Just wished, I guess."

Or you could invest, take business classes, learn a trade, make a budget, and spend wisely. Make steps toward your goal!

How much do we miss out on what the Lord wants to give us? What are we willing to believe about His generosity and treasures? We get discouraged if we pray for one person and that person does not get well. But what if we pray for 100? If one gets healed from cancer, is that worth it?

Keep on asking...keep on seeking...and keep on believing!

Ask, and it will be given to you;
seek, and you will find;
knock, and it will be opened to you.

MATTHEW 7:7

A quilt maker has the finished design in mind as she begins her work. As she chooses fabrics, patterns, and colors, she knows where she's headed. It's the end result that inspires her through the work of planning and stitching and cutting.

God knew where He was headed when He knitted you together. He had your whole life dreamed up. As He (who could snap you together in a moment) patiently formed your body over days and months, He daydreamed about who you would become. He looked forward to the very day you would choose to believe in Jesus. He smiled at the joy you would bring. And He put you together perfectly, piece by loving piece at a time. You, friend, are very much on purpose.

You formed my inward parts;
You wove me in my mother's womb.

PSALM 139:13

There's a reason the armor of God (Eph. 6:10-18) fits all the front pieces of our body, but not the back. We've got a breastplate of righteousness and a sword of the Spirit. We have a helmet of salvation and a shield of faith. But no back plate. Why? Because we are made for advancing in life! But we also need not look behind in fear. Because the Lord has our back. He keeps us protected from the front, the back, and on all sides. We do not fight alone. In fact, we are part of a great army of Saints, surrounded by the Lord's protection. So move forward confidently, and know that God has your back.

You have enclosed me behind and before, and laid Your hand upon me. Such knowledge is too wonderful for me; it is too high, I cannot attain to it.

PSALM 139:5-6

Remember our discussion on June 20 about the holdfast organ on certain sea plants? It's the reason those plants don't drift away with the tide.

Wherever you go, Jesus is your firm foundation. He serves as your security in new situations and places. It also means that there's no escaping the work He wants to do in your heart. Leaving a hard situation without dealing with the root cause won't solve the problem. That problem will follow you if it originates inside. But the Lord follows you too. He never stops caring about you or waiting to work. The best thing is to let Him deal with your root needs now, instead of running and hiding. He always knows right where you are.

If I take the wings of the dawn,
If I dwell in the remotest part of the sea,
even there Your hand will lead me,
And Your right hand will lay hold of me.
PSALM 139:9-10

Mr. Green was the coolest teacher in school. Everyone wanted him. He was not only skilled in teaching, but he was funny and full of life. He took special care with each of his students. And he always seemed to find some unique and crazy field trip to take them on.

When incoming fourth graders learned they had Mr. Green, most jumped up and cheered—and so did the parents! The year was bound to be great in Green's classroom.

We who have God as our Father can jump up and cheer too. What we have is the opportunity for so much growth, love, fun, and adventure in life. No one else has access to what we do—and we should be very excited about what we've been given!

Let all who take refuge in You be glad,
let them ever sing for joy;
and may You shelter them, that those
who love Your name may exult in You.

PSALM 5:11

"Joe! Don't ever forget to flip the safety valve again! You've got to do that every time you start the machine!" Joe thought Kevin's tone was harsh, and he wanted to be offended. But then his eyes slid down Kevin's arm to his right hand...which was missing a finger. Kevin had once told Joe how he had carelessly treated the bundling machine years ago, allowing his hand to get too close to the blades. Kevin's tone softened and he smiled. "I've been there, man. Just want you to keep all your digits."

Those who've been there, know. There are enough chances in life to figure things out on our own. But when we have a wise companion with us, it's a great idea to let them lead us.

It is better to listen to the rebuke of a wise man than for one to listen to the song of fools.

ECCLESIASTES 7:5

If you have a dog, chances are you've experienced some of the most loyal companionship known to man (or woman). A family dog is intent on being near. Call his name, and he will most likely come from around some corner (if he isn't in the room with you already) to see what's up. Open a familiar snack drawer, and he'll wake up from the deepest nap to keep you and your snack company. If you are working he may be at your feet, across the room, or beside you—but most likely within hearing distance.

Perhaps the Lord gave us dogs so that we could experience the trustworthy loyalty of calling His name, and knowing He is right there with us.

*The LORD is near to all who call upon Him,
to all who call upon Him in truth.*

PSALM 145:18

Knowledge is important. But without knowing how to apply it, that knowledge won't be very effective. Being and doing good are wonderful. But without the faith it takes to believe in God's plan for life and eternity, doing good is an empty task.

Jesus said that loving the Lord your God with all our heart, soul, and mind (Lk. 10:27) is the greatest command we have. Begin by believing in your heart that He is who He says He is. Then aim to live according to the good riches of the kingdom. Finally, use the knowledge you've gathered, and ask for more. Together these qualities will make you a powerful servant for His work.

Now for this very reason also, applying all diligence, in your faith supply moral excellence, and in your moral excellence, knowledge.

II PETER 1:5

The cross of Christ is an absolutely essential part of our existence as believers. Jesus' resurrection has meant a life-after-death experience for us. But some Christians get stuck there. They spend their lives living as sinners chained to the cross, unable to forget the horrible reason Jesus had to die in the first place.

When Jesus died, the veil was torn—our separation from the Father was no longer an issue. We were welcomed into His presence by grace alone.

The need to be reminded constantly of our freedom keeps us from living truly free. It's best to believe by faith that, yes! You are approved for the kingdom! Then you can move on and truly be an amazing force for His good.

Be diligent to present yourself approved to God as a workman who does not need to be ashamed, accurately handling the word of truth.

II TIMOTHY 2:15

It can be overwhelming to see all the need around us every day. Kids who don't eat unless schools provide lunches. Veterans with broken bodies, minds, or hearts. Young girls kidnapped and used in the sex trade. A person can feel useless and pointless in the midst of so much need.

The Lord thought ahead to this problem. He knows the needs. And He prepared your set of needs even before you were born. He knows where He wants you.

So how do you figure out where He wants you? Stay in tune. Be His partner. Pay attention to the things that stir your heart in a special way. Then go out in joy, and serve. He will show you the way.

For we are His workmanship, created in
Christ Jesus for good works,
which God prepared beforehand so that
we would walk in them.

EPHESIANS 2:10

Marching band musicians need not only learn the craft of their instrument, but they need to learn to march in step with dozens of others while playing memorized songs. At football halftime shows, the marchers show their hard work and preparation in forming shapes across the field with their bandmates.

One essential element of a good marching band is precision. A musician out of step is very obvious to anyone watching, because they are looking at the bigger picture.

The ways of the Spirit are specific and recognizable. Anyone who doesn't follow His lead will be out of step with the kingdom of God. But follow Him, and God's precise plans will contribute to the beautiful bigger picture.

If we live by the Spirit,
let us also walk by the Spirit.
GALATIANS 5:25

All she was doing was organizing her closet. And out of nowhere, a thought popped into her mind: I would love to visit Ireland someday. She'd never thought it before. But right then, it was suddenly a real dream!

A week later she got a call from a close friend. "Our church is taking a mission trip to Northern Ireland next year. Would you be interested in joining us?"

When a person dedicates her life to following Jesus, one of the things He does is to adapt our heart's desires to His own. It's not unlike Him to plant desires in our hearts, just so that He can have the pleasure of fulfilling them. He loves to delight those who delight in Him.

Delight yourself in the LORD;
and He will give you the desires of your heart.

PSALM 37:4

He steps up to the starting line behind many other, faster-looking, more professionally dressed looking runners. This hasn't been his best training year, due to injuries early on and a busy work schedule. But he has always enjoyed running.

Success, he said to Holy Spirit under his breath, is not to run my fastest race today. Success is to run with You, to have fun, and I would like to run this half marathon in under two hours. Let's do this!

Define success with the Holy Spirit, not according to the world's standards—and you'll live a much happier, more satisfied life. Then enjoy the journey. You may be surprised at what His ideas of success really are.

May He grant you your heart's desire and fulfill all your counsel!

PSALM 20:4

*L*ots of people start lots of projects. And lots of projects fall by the wayside. That blanket you began knitting three years ago, still in balls of yarn. The photos you were going to organize for your daughter before she graduates. Your early enthusiasm to learn graphic design in your spare time. Beginning is the easy part.

Most people get waylaid in the follow-through. Staying committed is hard, because staying committed takes patience. And patience is a fruit of the Spirit. And the Spirit needs time and a practice field in order for patience to grow.

Maybe that thing you started is exactly the field He wanted to use to grow your patience and endurance. Maybe beginning again would yield most tastily fruitful results!

The end of a matter is better than its beginning; Patience of spirit is better than haughtiness of spirit.

ECCLESIASTES 7:8

Faith. By very definition, in order to have faith we need to be blind to the future. Because if we could see the road ahead, it wouldn't be faith—it would be knowing!

Faith is the evidence of things not seen. It's great to know what's coming. But it is grand to take steps forward, believing God, trusting in His promises.

Want to be bold? Try asking God to keep you unaware of the next steps in the road. Maybe you'll put your house on the market and sell it before you know where you're moving to. Or maybe you'll buy baby clothes long before you get pregnant. Whatever your area of faith, it will bless the Lord. And it will surely bless you too.

For we walk by faith,
not by sight.
II CORINTHIANS 5:7

What if the only way to get to Hawaii were to build a land bridge across the ocean? Most certainly, no one would visit Hawaii. It is simply impossible to build a bridge that far across, with no supports.

What if the only way to get to God were to live absolutely perfect lives? No support or help, across a chasm of sin and temptation? Most certainly, no one would make it into the arms of the Father.

But with Jesus, records of sin are erased. We start with a clean slate, washed pure and white and clean. And as we go, repentance and rest bring us new hope and new mercy. Forgiveness is surely one of the greatest (and most necessary) gifts of God.

If You, LORD, should mark iniquities, O Lord, who could stand? But there is forgiveness with You, that You may be feared.

PSALM 130:3-4

God is more than the inventor of love. He is more than the One who keeps love going. God is love. Every characteristic that can be applied to love, can be applied to God. He is not rude or self-seeking. He is not easily angered. He keeps no record of wrongs.

When we love others, we're actually living out God's character. And when we are full of emotion, confused and hurt, and need to be reminded of how to love someone in this situation...we can examine God's character. We can mine First Corinthians 13 to look for help. And if we follow that way, we will never, ever go wrong.

Love is patient, love is kind and is not jealous;
love does not brag and is not arrogant,
does not act unbecomingly; it does not seek its
own, is not provoked, does not take
into account a wrong suffered.

1 CORINTHIANS 13:4-5

John 14:23 can be read two different ways: If you love Me, you'll do what I say. Or, Your love for me will be evident through the way you follow Me.

Love is often noticed by the way we treat others. It's hard to be kind, compassionate, and generous when we're full of anger or hate. But when we're brimming with hope and love, our kindness tends to overflow from our hearts into the world around us.

Jesus doesn't command us because it makes Him feel good. His commands are for our benefit, and sometimes they are more like observations and wisdom for us to live by.

Jesus answered and said to him, "If anyone loves Me, he will keep My word; and My Father will love him, and We will come to him and make Our abode with him."

JOHN 14:23

Some bosses are helicopter bosses. They love to hover over their employees, watching every move and giving their input. Other bosses are hands-off bosses. They're around and available, but won't come to you unless they're needed.

Jesus is a loving leader boss. He's a perfect example, a servant, a helper and a prayer warrior on your behalf. He wants you to succeed and will step in when the time is right. But He also keeps a close distance as you work things out on your own. He rewards your efforts and successes, and forgives the mistakes. And in the end, the wages He pays will be ridiculously above market average.

For the Son of Man is going to come in the glory of His Father with His angels, and will then repay every man according to his deeds.

MATTHEW 16:27

Several years ago, a man emerged into the public eye claiming he was the Messiah. He gathered several followers, and they lived in a closed-off compound near the wilderness. He claimed that he was the answer to all things—a savior. Sadly, the man convinced his followers to drink a poisoned beverage together. They were found in their beds by authorities—and that was the end of the group.

There is no one but God. No name other than Jesus. And no other promise for hope, joy, peace, fulfilment and freedom. Men may deceive, and the Bible warns us of this possibility. But stick with Jesus and you will be living forever with Him.

And there is salvation in no one else; for there is no other name under heaven that has been given among men by which we must be saved.

ACTS 4:12

"If you clean your rooms, I'll take you for ice cream later!" Annika says, "Sure, I'll do it after this show!" Caylie grumbles, "Aw, man, cleaning is lame." Caylie shuffles off to her room. An hour later, she emerges to show Mom her tidy space. Annika, however, is still watching television three hours later. Mom calls, "Goodbye honey, I'm taking Caylie to ice cream!"

"But Mom! Caylie's attitude was stinky about it!"

"You said you would clean, but you didn't. The reward is for those who do the work!"

God knows us well enough not to be surprised or offended by our emotions and struggles. But in the end, the reward will be for those who profess Jesus and follow His leading.

Not everyone who says to Me,
"Lord, Lord," will enter the kingdom of heaven,
but he who does the will of My Father
who is in heaven will enter.

MATTHEW 7:21

Try going on a treasure hunt. One through the Bible, to discover what it looks like to love the Lord with all your mind. You may come upon 2 Corinthians 10:5, about taking every thought captive that sets itself up against God. You might float through the Psalms, discovering the ways that David pondered the bigness of the night sky as he laid awake with his sheep. You'll probably dwell in Philippians 4:8 with Paul for a while, thinking through what true, right, noble, lovely, pure, excellent, praiseworthy things there are to think about. Wherever you end up, the Bible is full of suggestions for giving God your whole mind.

And He said to him, "You shall love the Lord your God with all your heart, and with all your soul, and with all your mind."

MATTHEW 22:37

Wrath is "the just punishment of an offense or crime" (Webster's 1828 Dictionary).

Wrath is known as anger or violence. It is also about justice. The cross of Christ, and the sacrifice the Father made for us, is the supreme example of both. The cross was a violent act. Nothing about it was tame or easy. But it wasn't pointed at us. It happened for us.

There is nothing just about the cross, if you frame it in terms of what we deserve. We did not deserve the substitution Jesus made, putting Himself in place of sin. But the cross gave us grace, so that we might have a chance at salvation.

Yes, God is a wrathful God. And we would not want it any other way.

For God has not destined us for wrath, but for obtaining salvation through our Lord Jesus Christ, who died for us, so that whether we are awake or asleep, we will live together with Him. Therefore encourage one another and build up one another, just as you also are doing.

I THESSALONIANS 5:9-11

You follow her to the back door of the stage, wondering if this is going to work. You met this stranger just a few minutes before, as you spoke excitedly in the lobby about the lead actor of the play you just saw. She knocks on the door. A uniformed man opens. He looks you over once. Then he turns to the woman. "Ma'am," he nods in my direction. "Is she with you?"

Your new acquaintance smiles. "Yes, we're here to see my dad." At that, the two of you walk straight through security.

You have an advocate for you, and His name is Jesus. Because He is intimately acquainted with the Father, you have access to the throne of heaven. Jesus vouches for you.

To this end also we pray for you always, that our God will count you worthy of your calling, and fulfill every desire for goodness and the work of faith with power.

II THESSALONIANS 1:11

God is many things, not the least of which is love. He is all-powerful, meaning nothing can outdo Him. He is uncreated, meaning no one came before Him. He is everywhere, meaning nothing happens on earth or in heaven outside of His jurisdiction.

But above it all, God is love. We know His justice and faithfulness. But a just God without love would be hard and cold. And a faithful God could faithfully show up, but without compassion or comfort. God's love is what warms us from the inside out. His character of love is what allows us to feel loved and give love. God's plan is hinged on His incredible love for each of us.

Your kingdom is an everlasting kingdom,
and Your dominion endures
throughout all generations.

PSALM 145:13

Jesus wasn't tempted by sexual sin...right? Or maybe it was murder. He was never tempted to imagine a terrible end for someone who was mean to Him...right? No. Jesus was tempted in every way. Every opportunity was there for Him to make a wrong move and choose sin.

Well it must have been easy for Him, because He was man and God...right? But Jesus made Himself fully man. He had no secret stash of superhero strength. However, He did have a supernatural relationship of grace with His Father.

Everything He had...both hard and good...belongs to us too. All the grace you need to make it through. It hinges on your relationship with the King.

For we do not have a high priest
who cannot sympathize with our weaknesses,
but One who has been tempted
in all things as we are, yet without sin.

HEBREWS 4:15

Rules for Pasadena Tournament of Roses New Year's Day parade dictate that every visual element of each float be made of living things. Every inch of a float's surface is covered with seeds, beans, dried and fresh flowers.

As the parade slowly passes, each float gives off a unique scent-mix of the organic materials it's made up of. Watchers leave the parade with the scent of roses in their noses all day long.

We are the fragrance of Christ. Everywhere we go, we give off the scent of Jesus. The more inundated we are in His presence, the more of His beautiful fragrance we give off to the world.

But thanks be to God, who always leads us in triumph in Christ, and manifests through us the sweet aroma of the knowledge of Him in every place.

II CORINTHIANS 2:14

He had acted out. Again. Graffiti on the gym wall. The teacher and principal met, and came to an agreement about what to do with the unruly student.

The boy walked into the principal's office, feet shuffling. "Chris, it's the third time this month. It should be your final warning, and grounds for suspension. But I know your home life isn't easy right now. We care about you. So instead of suspension, we have a special project for you. That gym wall you keep tagging? It actually needs a really great mural painted on it....

Mercy is receiving a reward that directly opposes what our actions deserve. God is the God of mercy and loving-kindness.

Blessed be the God and Father of our Lord Jesus Christ, who according to His great mercy has caused us to be born again to a living hope through the resurrection of Jesus Christ from the dead.

I PETER 1:3

When a family's lease agreement is up after 12 months, a new one is written. It's a new agreement—not nullifying the old, but continuing the agreement on fresh terms.

God made a Law covenant with Moses. The Law was a clear illustration that people could never be pure enough to be in God's presence. He is too holy.

Some people struggle with the idea that a new covenant was made by Jesus' resurrection. Does that mean God went back on His word with Moses?

Think of the new covenant of Jesus' blood—grace and mercy—as a fulfillment of the old covenant of Law. Think of it as, "Oh, that's how we can draw near to the Holy of Holies. Jesus!"

*When you were dead in your transgressions
and the uncircumcision of your flesh,
He made you alive together with Him,
having forgiven us all our transgressions.*

COLOSSIANS 2:13-14

Sometimes a loved one hurts you many times over by their actions. Forgiveness every time will do your heart much good.

Sometimes, though, a wound by one person goes deep. You may forgive them once and want to be completely good with them—but the pain is still there. It can take a very long time to work through feelings of betrayal, rejection, or shame.

In those cases, forgiveness may need to happen every day. Every time you pray. Every time the pain is worst. As warfare—to protect your own heart from bitterness, and to protect your relationship with the person.

Seventy times seven may seem like a lot. But if you've been there, you know. Forgiving deep hurts can be a marathon, more than a sprint.

Then Peter came and said to Him, "Lord, how often shall my brother sin against me and I forgive him? Up to seven times?" Jesus said to him, "I do not say to you, up to seven times, but up to seventy times seven."

MATTHEW 18:21-22

*L*ife in Christ is an ongoing process. It's not your job to fix yourself—although at times of major frustration, that may be exactly what you want to do.

But it's the job of the Holy Spirit to work in you. Your job is to surrender. Be open, pliable, raw, honest and available. The Holy Spirit is the Master Gardener with all the tools to plough and plant. He transforms weedy vines into fruitful trees.

As much as your Father forgives you, loves you, and shows you mercy—receive it, and offer that same grace to yourself. Jesus commanded us to love our neighbor as much as we love ourselves. That requires that we do love ourselves! Because He first loved us.

*For the good that I want, I do not do,
but I practice the very evil that I do not want.*

ROMANS 7:19

The tourists stood in awe at the gigantic elephant—powerful and strong, but tied by a thin rope around its front foot. They wondered, "Why doesn't he break free? He could easily snap that cord!"

"This beast is my friend," the elephant's caretaker said. "He ran away often when he was a baby, so he was tied by a thin rope to a post. He tried and tried to escape, but the rope was too strong. Over time he stopped trying. And to this day, he believes that he is helplessly bound."

One of the saddest sights is a Christian who is still enslaved to his past. Because of Jesus, power was given to you to serve God in the world. You can break free!

I have been crucified with Christ; and it is no longer I who live, but Christ lives in me; and the life which I now live in the flesh I live by faith in the Son of God, who loved me and gave Himself up for me.

GALATIANS 2:20

Unlike most plants and flowers, the seed of bitterness needs darkness to grow. It shivers in the daylight, and thrives in the dark.

The very best thing to do, when you've been offended, is to forgive. Release all offenders from the responsibility of making things right with you. Ask the Lord for help. Even tell that seed of bitterness, "I see you. I'm not going to let you take root. Go away!"

Bitterness won't stay where it's not wanted. Especially if you throw the scalding water of truth at its roots. It can't stand to be seen with the truth of God.

Be angry, and yet do not sin;
do not let the sun go down on your anger,
and do not give the devil an opportunity.
EPHESIANS 4:26-27

In this age we have all sorts of tools and implements designed to bring us a sense of safety. Our cars and homes have alarm systems. Our airports have extensive policies about traveling safely. Even babies carry fuzzy blankets to help them feel safe! There's nothing wrong with making plans to live wisely. But as far as where our trust lies, that only belongs in one place.

David had a word of wisdom: "Some trust in chariots and some trust in horses," he sang, "but we trust in the name of the Lord our God." Or this from Solomon, the wisest man in history: "The horse is prepared for the day of battle, but victory belongs to the Lord."

My soul, wait in silence for God only,
for my hope is from Him. He only is my rock
and my salvation, My stronghold;
I shall not be shaken.

PSALM 62:5-6

In the very name of God is the fact of His promise to give you all you need. Jehovah Jireh: God Our Provider. And since He never goes back on His word, know that you will never lack for the necessities.

Things may not be easy. The Lord may lead you through seasons of trusting Him completely and against all odds, because character is grown in desert times. But you can truly sing with rejoicing, because it's in the times of most-needed faith that you learn the most and grow the strongest.

Trust Him, seek Him, follow Him even through the valleys—and Jehovah Jireh will lead you to abundant places!

Then the LORD said to Moses, "Behold, I will rain bread from heaven for you; and the people shall go out and gather a day's portion every day, that I may test them, whether or not they will walk in My instruction."

EXODUS 16:4

When you feel overwhelmed, confused, and hurt, a natural tendency is to withdraw. You can do that two ways. Withdrawing from community, away from the support and love God has surrounded you with, is what the enemy would like you to do. He aims to isolate you so that he can whisper lies and no one can counteract those lies with truth.

Another way to withdraw is into the shadow of the Almighty God. There, you can rest in His protection. You can cry out for help. You can cry, yell, and feel all the feelings. You can ask for advice from wise loved ones.

Withdraw into the arms of God, and you will find a peace that passes understanding.

But you, when you pray, go into your inner room, close your door and pray to your Father who is in secret, and your Father who sees what is done in secret will reward you.

MATTHEW 6:6

A zebra has gotten stuck in quicksand. People have brought boards for the zebra to step on, and tied ropes around his neck to help pull him forward. But the zebra panics. The more he struggles, the more he sinks.

One man squats in front of the zebra and speaks quietly. "Be still, friend. We're here to help." After a few minutes, the zebra settles down. The helpers are able to tug him gently forward, until his hoof finds a solid wood. From there the zebra gains confidence and assists the helpers to lead him out of danger.

In the face of trouble, there is a wise One who leans in and whispers peace. Be still, and know that He is God.

This poor man cried, and the LORD heard him and saved him out of all his troubles.

PSALM 34:6

Most superhero alliances include one member who has unlimited monetary resources. This provides the opportunity for us to feel that the possibilities are absolutely endless where buying things is concerned! Wealthy people can act like superheroes if they can buy the best materials for a super-suit, and build the most tricked out vehicles or weapons.

We instinctively understand the value of unlimited resources. Perhaps this is because we are designed to understand that God's resources, in every sense, are one hundred percent limitless!

What help do you need from our limitless God today?

And my God will supply all your needs according to His riches in glory in Christ Jesus.

PHILIPPIANS 4:19

*B*ehold: the cereal aisle. Fifty glorious feet of every color, shape, and flavor of sugary goodness. Or if you prefer: gluten free grains, sugarless oats, and athlete-approved flakes for all. If you can imagine a box made for milk and mornings, it probably exists at a store in your city.

We love choices! And if we don't see what we want, we make our own!

Although cereal hasn't been around since the beginning, the desire for independence has. People have searched for answers other than God. But there is only One. No other god can hold a candle to the Alpha and Omega.

Some choices are harmless. But sometimes, the very best choice is the only One that makes sense.

For from days of old they have not heard or perceived by ear, nor has the eye seen a God besides You, who acts in behalf of the one who waits for Him.

ISAIAH 64:4

Finals were a week away, and he was looking at his schedule wondering how in the world he would survive. Maybe if he skipped church on Sunday, ignored friends and phone calls, and stayed up all night....

"Lord, I can't do this. I admit it. But I know You can. So I'm giving You my schedule and all that's on my plate for the next two weeks. Just tell me: What's my next step?"

So he did the next thing. And then the next. And then the next. And little by little, he got through with God on his side.

God isn't asking you to solve life. He's asking you to focus on His face, and just do the next thing.

So do not worry about tomorrow;
for tomorrow will care for itself.
Each day has enough trouble of its own.
MATTHEW 6:34

The very definition of faith includes the requirement that you not be able to see into the future. If you could, then it wouldn't be faith, which is "the substance of things hoped for; the evidence of things not seen" (Hebrews 11:1). Faith means trusting God for the path ahead; trusting He is good and knowing He knows better than we do. Another element of faith is to not worry, which is an attempt to control the uncontrollable. Our most important job, in times of the unknown, is to keep our eyes on Jesus and follow His lead.

Declaring the end from the beginning, and from ancient times things which have not been done, Saying, "My purpose will be established, and I will accomplish all My good pleasure."

ISAIAH 46:10

To be forgiven. Offenses forgotten. A do-over every time you ask. A clean slate and a fresh start. New mercy today that didn't exist last night.

Do you believe it? Do you receive it? Can you handle the fact that He doesn't hold one single thing against you? Yes, friend...even that thing. The one no one knows about. If you've decided to change your mind about it (repentance), then He has too. If you haven't yet and are still holding on, now is the time. Trust His love, even though you don't understand it. Take your tears and pain. He knows the root of all that. And He can heal. He wants to, in fact.

> I, even I, am the one who wipes out your
> transgressions for My own sake,
> and I will not remember your sins.
>
> ISAIAH 43:25

The couple had worked so hard for the past two years to pay off their debt. The debt that had just sort of appeared over time, through mistakes and lack of trust and further education. And still, as they looked at their budget, things seemed hopeless. Prayer had become their strategy as they continued to pay things off one dollar at a time.

One day a man approached them at church. "I have something for you. I believe the Lord has asked me to pay off your balance. Bills, house, student loans, everything. Tell me what you owe and I will pay. I won't take no for an answer."

God's grace is truly overwhelming, and miracles are not outdated. Keep praying, keep working, and keep believing. You never know how He'll show up.

As sin reigned in death, even so grace would reign through righteousness to eternal life through Jesus Christ our Lord.

ROMANS 5:21

There's always a reason for God's discipline. His justice, even toward your character, is worth the temporary discomfort. The wise person who experiences His discipline will lean in even closer to hear Him. "I don't want to go through this again, so teach me all You have for me to learn this time around. Thank You for loving me so much to show me the way."

The unwise person, on the other hand, looks for excuses and escapes. She will most likely end up "learning" the same lesson over and over again.

Discipline lasts for a short season; shorter if you're a fast learner. The freedom and joy of maturity will last forever.

Who is a God like You, who pardons iniquity and passes over the rebellious act of the remnant of His possession? He does not retain His anger forever, because He delights in unchanging love.

MICAH 7:18

After 30 years of membership, the old club member had died. He had shown up faithfully every month and was well liked, but no one had any idea....

In the months that followed, task after task surfaced undone around the organization. The plants were dying. The coffee was horrible. Dust bunnies filled the corners of the meeting room.

People gradually caught on: the humble old club member had been serving in countless silent ways.

Are you the type who serves, or the type who prefers to be served? Do you want to be seen for your work, or do you enjoy going unnoticed? It matters little in the end: but true sacrifice is seen by God, and that's the thing to delight in.

Greater love has no one than this,
that one lay down his life for his friends.
JOHN 15:13

There were many sick people in Jesus' day, but He didn't heal them all. It wasn't His modus operandi to seek out all lame and diseased people.

Jesus did consistently heal in two ways, however. First, if people came to Him. In every instance we know of, He healed their bodies. Second, Jesus knew that spiritual sickness was just as urgent (if not more so) as physical sickness. "It is not those who are healthy who need a physician, but those who are sick; I did not come to call the righteous, but sinners." (Mk. 2:17)

Stay in tune with the Father, and then pay attention to the people who cross your path. You may have just the touch they need to be well.

While the sun was setting, all those who had any who were sick with various diseases brought them to Him; and laying His hands on each one of them, He was healing them.

LUKE 4:40

Knowledge is different from wisdom. Knowledge can come from textbooks and Google searches. But with wisdom, knowing and understanding go hand in hand. True wisdom requires the Holy Spirit to help a person see where his knowledge fits in the context of life.

Every experience you have can lead to the wisdom of God, if you ask for it and keep your eyes open. If any of you lacks wisdom, let him ask of God, who gives to all generously and without reproach, and it will be given to him (James 1:5). To be a truly wise person, we have the formula: Fear God, follow Him, and that not a single moment of your life be wasted.

The fear of the LORD is the beginning
of wisdom; a good understanding have
all those who do His commandments;
His praise endures forever.

PSALM 111:10

He was the first founder of DaySpring to pass away. His last days were some of the sweetest a person could wish to experience. In fact, being in his presence felt like a true honor and privilege. Although he could barely speak or stay awake, "Hallelujah!" or "Praise the Lord!" often appeared on his lips. He smiled often. It was clear he was at peace.

His last words, before his final step into heaven, were, "This is so much fun!"

A life in God's hands leads to the most profound peace, a peace unlike the kind the world gives.

But godliness actually is a means of great gain when accompanied by contentment.

I TIMOTHY 6:6

Have you ever said the words, "If I'd known what I was getting into before I started, I wouldn't have started!"? And yet, you may have had a sense of confidence that you were right where God wanted you. How is that? Does He make a habit of leading us into big fat mistakes?

It's more likely that God protects us from knowing some challenges ahead, because He knows we have a strong instinct for self-protection. His grace is far beyond our understanding. It's hard to imagine, before we get there, that we'll be able to get through some tough circumstances. But God knows. He always prepares enough grace for the moment. And the reward for following His lead is worth aiming for!

Whatever you do, do your work heartily,
as for the Lord rather than for men,
knowing that from the Lord you will receive
the reward of the inheritance. It is
the Lord Christ whom you serve.

COLOSSIANS 3:23-24

"But why didn't you come to me?" A long string of gossip had led to the widespread belief that Julie was going to fire multiple people within the week. As soon as she heard about it, Julie went to the source. The frustrated employee finally explained that he'd messed up on a project, and expected Julie would be mad. So he had lashed out behind her back instead of talking with her. "I just didn't know what to say to you."

Prayer only works when we go to Him. The same rules apply as with people: Be honest, listen well, and have a humble heart. The Holy Spirit is there for the express purpose of mediating the conversation: there's never anything to be afraid to take to God.

In the same way the Spirit also helps our weakness; for we do not know how to pray as we should, but the Spirit Himself intercedes for us with groanings too deep for words;

ROMANS 8:26

Have you ever had an advocate: Someone who has your very best interest in mind? Maybe it was a teacher who intervened in a home situation. Maybe it is a friend or spouse who always represents you well when talking to others. An advocate knows you, cares about you, and represents you better than you represent yourself sometimes!

The Spirit is such an advocate. He talks to the Father about you. He builds you up and represents you well! He is not in the business of making you look bad, but of noticing your God-given gifts and assets and bringing those to light. Rest in peace today—because Someone is fighting for you.

He who searches the hearts knows what the mind of the Spirit is, because He intercedes for the saints according to the will of God.

ROMANS 8:27

911, what's your emergency?

"Help! I totally screwed up with my kids today. I yelled at them and disciplined them when they didn't deserve it. I think they hate me!"

Stay calm, ma'am. Nothing is broken beyond repair. Stay on the line with me and let's talk to the Father together. And don't worry! He loves to answer these 911 emergencies!

God is not in the ignoring-needs business. The fact that you call on Him is a delight to His heart. Imagine how He may feel! Yippee, she trusts me to handle even this situation. This is wonderful! I can't wait to step in.

The next time you start to panic, remember to hit the panic button of prayer.

Call upon Me in the day of trouble;
I shall rescue you, and you will honor Me.
PSALM 50:15

Forget your station. Forget your title. Forget what you're wearing today, who knows you exist, how much money you make, or what kind of bicycle you ride.

At the core, we are all sheep. We all flock together. We all follow the same Shepherd. Some of us wear wool suits, and some of us wear woolen underwear. But wool is wool, and once in a while we are all subject to being shorn.

Do you think that in a real flock, much time is spent comparing nose color or hoof size or who is eating the better patch of grass? No! Every sheep has its place in the shepherd's presence. Life is good, when you're a sheep in the kingdom of God.

How precious is Your lovingkindness, O God! And the children of men take refuge in the shadow of Your wings. They drink their fill of the abundance of Your house; and You give them to drink of the river of Your delights.

PSALM 36:7-8

About halfway through the garage sale, she noticed that the crystal flutes were gone. No one had paid for them.

At first she was angry. Someone stole from me! That's so unfair! But she prayed. Lord, it makes me mad that people would steal! Help me have your attitude about this. She felt peace about just letting it go.

Many years later, a man came knocking on her door. "Ma'am, I once stole some glasses from your garage sale. I was in a bad place, and I am so sorry. Here is the money for them, plus some extra for interest.

Nothing escapes the Lord's sight, and He will work all things for His glory. Just hang tight and watch Him do His thing.

Be gracious to me, O God, according to Your lovingkindness; according to the greatness of Your compassion blot out my transgressions. ...Against You, You only, I have sinned and done what is evil in Your sight, so that You are justified when You speak and blameless when You judge.

PSALM 51:1, 4

The word "amusement" comes from two root words: a, meaning "no;" and muse, meaning "think." In other words, the point of amusement is to not think!

There is nothing wrong with having fun. In fact, fun is part of God's character! But we've all probably had the mindset of doing something to just "check out" for a while.

If diversions are a lifestyle for you, it may be wise to ask the Lord if you're in balance. He'll let you know if you're on the right path. Remember, every single moment of life serves a purpose for His kingdom. You are desperately needed—your laughter, spunk, tenderness, compassion, and whatever gifts He has given you. Not a moment of your life is wasted, in His book.

So teach us to number our days,
that we may present to You a heart of wisdom.

PSALM 90:12

Sometimes it's so helpful to hear, You're doing a good job! A mom of teens needs to hear that often. A husband needs to know he's a good provider and protector. A pastor needs to be reminded that his care and commitment are serving the kingdom beautifully.

There are many more people along a marathon route than just the runners. Spectators hold signs and cowbells, yelling encouragement. At stations for water, the "keep going, you're doing great!" messages of the volunteers make a big difference.

Let's face it, life's tough! We can wonder if we're really making a mark for good. Learn from the apostle Paul, who took time to write "Keep on doing what you're doing," and go encourage someone today.

But you are to cling to the LORD your God, as you have done to this day.

JOSHUA 23:8

Acertain family has spent recent years in the television spotlight. As of this writing, they have 19 children whose names all begin with the same letter. Can you imagine if, at some point, the parents could not remember how many children they have? What if one child were forgotten at a store and never searched for, because no one remembered? Unthinkable! Every one of those children is loved and known.

God, who is infinitely more knowledgeable, would never forget one of His children. He would never let one be unnamed. He is keenly aware of every single detail of every single life. You needn't go to Him and expect to be misunderstood. In fact, He's the only one who really, truly gets you!

But the very hairs of your head
are all numbered.

MATTHEW 10:30

This time things were different. Joshua, not Moses, stood at the edge of the water, needing to cross over (Jos. 3:7-17). The Israelites were not running for their lives, this time. It may have taken more coaxing for the people to trust that this would work. But they had testimony. They remembered that God had parted an even bigger body of water than the Jordan River, and their lives had been saved because of it. So they stepped in.

Remembering what God has done can build faith that He will do it again. Listening to others' stories can strengthen your own. What do you need to see happen? Seek out others who've been there before... and soak in the truth of His ability.

The LORD appeared to him from afar, saying,
"I have loved you with an everlasting love;
therefore I have drawn you
with lovingkindness."

JEREMIAH 31:3

It's amazing what a person can do with a board, a speed boat, and a body of water. The best skiers can leap, spin, and even carry others on their shoulders! All of this would be impossible (or at least, way less exciting) if the boat didn't have a wake.

The wake is the displaced water behind a speeding boat. It creates turbulence that the skier learns to use in his favor.

The Lord promises that as you follow Him, kindness and mercy will come along behind you. Everywhere you go, as you ooze the love of Jesus, you'll create waves. See if you can spot it today: Good work of the Lord in the lives of the people around you, may just be the wake of His presence.

Surely goodness and lovingkindness will follow me all the days of my life, and I will dwell in the house of the LORD forever.

PSALM 23:6

There's nothing quite like being rejected. It's hard! We are made for connection and community, so the mere idea of a broken connection goes against our grain.

But we know that life has hard things. Jesus promised, in fact (Jn. 16:33). We can count on difficulty coming our way, and that it's no surprise to Him.

Jesus has been there. He knows rejection on a deeper level, and in more brutal ways than we will ever experience in our lifetime. But He also received the King's reward in the end.

Stay strong, friend. Look to Jesus. Cry out to Him and remember, everything turns out victorious in the end.

For consider Him who has endured such hostility by sinners against Himself, so that you will not grow weary and lose heart.

HEBREWS 12:3

At around 17 weeks' gestation, a human baby is able to hear the sound of her mother's voice. She can recognize the soft droning, and even singing, from within the womb. That's a very early start!

God knew us even before we were in the womb (Jer. 1:5)! He has been speaking to us since the very beginning. In fact, it's the mere fact of His voice—His very breath of life—that creates our existence. So the idea that we wouldn't know His voice is even less probable than a child forgetting what her mother's voice sounds like.

Jesus doesn't say we can hear His voice; He says we do. Listen closely...what is He saying to you right now?

My sheep hear My voice, and I know them, and they follow Me.

JOHN 10:27

Consider the difference between calling and sending. A person doing the sending stays at the point of origin. He says, I'll stay here. You go there. Let it be well with you.

A person doing the calling says, I am here. Will you come here too? I can't wait to see you.

The Bible says that the Spirit calls us and leads us. He never sends us on ahead to a place He hasn't been. Instead, He invites us into His presence, in a new place, that He has prepared just for our situation. You can be confident that, if you're following His lead, you're not going alone and you won't ever be alone when you get there.

To him the doorkeeper opens, and the sheep hear his voice, and he calls his own sheep by name and leads them out. When he puts forth all his own, he goes ahead of them, and the sheep follow him because they know his voice.

JOHN 10:3-4

Your toddler wanders into the kitchen. "Hungee."

"You want something to eat, dear? Okay, there's a box of mac and cheese in the pantry. Use the stepladder to reach the milk on the top shelf. Careful not to step on the heating element when you climb the stove to turn it on."

That's probably not how things would go at your house! So, why do we assume that as God's children we are different?

We were never meant to lose our tenderness and innocence before God. He needs no tough, hardened heart from you. He invites you to be raw and vulnerable. In fact, that's when He does His best work.

Look at the birds of the air, that they do not sow, nor reap nor gather into barns, and yet your heavenly Father feeds them. Are you not worth much more than they?

MATTHEW 6:26

There are two ways to live in this world, at the risk of sounding a bit like a Shakespeare play: to do, and to be. Fitting ourselves into culture, acting like everyone else, that is us doing the doing. Letting the Lord lead us through culture, loving everyone around us, that is Him doing the transforming.

It's a bit like driving a car vs. being a passenger. We can take the wheel and be responsible for all of the road hazards and safe driving, or we can enjoy the scenery and go where He takes us.

Either way, things get done. The question is whose things, in what order, and according to which agenda. God's is always the best and most enjoyable!

And do not be conformed to this world, but be transformed by the renewing of your mind, so that you may prove what the will of God is, that which is good and acceptable and perfect.

ROMANS 12:2

It never offends God when we trust Him. Think of John the Baptist, reaching out to Jesus from prison. "Are you the Messiah?" (Lk. 7:19) He needed to know if his job had been accomplished; if his time was near.

Jesus answered his plea with a simple phrase: "Blessed is he who does not take offense at me." Perhaps He was thinking, Take heart, dear cousin. You have trusted Me enough to ask. And for that you are blessed. Things aren't easy for you, but they are about to be infinitely better. Your faith has been noticed by your Father in heaven.

Asking questions isn't doubting God, if in asking you believe He has the answer.

The LORD will accomplish what concerns me;
Your lovingkindness, O LORD, is everlasting;
do not forsake the works of Your hands.

PSALM 138:8

Think of a mother with a tender heart. She watches her child on the playground, smiling at the giggles and bounces. She whips her phone out to video the first successful crossing of the monkey bars. Good job, sweetie!! This mother kisses the scraped knee and uses the bandages with the child's favorite cartoon, which she bought for just an occasion like this. She sings soothing songs that put the child to sleep each night.

Life with the Lord is full of tender moments, as He lavishes His love on us. It's easy to think of Him as big and strong and powerful and Holy, which He certainly is. But He also has a mother's touch for our gentle, childlike heart.

The LORD your God is in your midst,
a victorious warrior. He will exult over you
with joy, He will be quiet in His love,
He will rejoice over you with shouts of joy.

ZEPHANIAH 3:17

The water boy has one job: Hydration.

He doesn't suit up and learn plays. He doesn't lift weights with the team. He simply shows up and carries cups. His job is to watch for thirsty players coming off the field, and allow them to refuel with electrolytes and water. It's a simple task. But dehydration would bring a hot, sweaty player down fast.

The Lord watches for His faithful players too. He carries the refreshment we need, and eagerly fills our cup when we need it. He proudly thinks, That's my team! as victory takes place on our field. Look for Him when your resources are low, and you'll surely feel strengthened soon.

For the eyes of the LORD move to and fro throughout the earth that He may strongly support those whose heart is completely His.

II CHRONICLES 16:9

You might be the first in your family who is a believer, or just the next in line. You might be the one who is hoping that your children or grandchildren will choose Jesus. In any case, we know that belief in Him always carries an impact to those around us. He is the Sower of very good seeds, and your life is like a spreader. Stay connected to Him and those seeds will go out wherever you walk and live.

It's up to Him to water those seeds. He might use you, or other people you don't even know. The Holy Spirit will always stir up the soil of faith when the time is right.

For I am mindful of the sincere faith within you, which first dwelt in your grandmother Lois and your mother Eunice, and I am sure that it is in you as well.

II TIMOTHY 1:5

Builders use a plumb line to make sure their lines are straight. Anchor one end to a foundation, carry the other end to the destination, and snap a chalk-covered string across the space in between. A line of blue appears—a straight line the builder can be sure of.

People and the world are constantly changing. Some of it is moving toward chaos. Some of it, as in the case of believers with the Holy Spirit, is being transformed to look more and more like Jesus Himself.

But the only thing to be sure of is Jesus, the One who never changes. Any other plumb line has a shaky foundation or a crooked board here and there. But Jesus can be trusted as sure as a straight chalk line.

Jesus Christ is the same yesterday
and today and forever.
HEBREWS 13:8

Watching those apocalyptic movies can be tough! No one likes to see iconic buildings being blown up by aliens or stepped on by monsters. Sometimes when the White House crumbles or a Hawaiian island explodes, it's easy to forget that this is just the cinematic creation of an imaginative director.

At the same time, there is a reality reflected in those movies. We live in a world that will disappear. But that's not a threat; it's a promise!

Our new world will be brilliant. We'll live a resurrected life in the presence of the Son. The light of day will come straight from Him! Have you ever taken time to imagine what eternity will look like? It will be better than any movie could ever hope to depict.

For here we do not have a lasting city,
but we are seeking the city which is to come.
HEBREWS 13:14

What if everywhere you went, this big dude in a black muscle shirt stared angrily at every passerby, bumping little old ladies' shopping carts out of the way so you could pass? You probably wouldn't have very many friends!

But, what if you really do have a bodyguard? And what if it looks a lot more like feeling peace when it doesn't make sense, or people bending over backwards to love you when you need it? What if your joy ran so deep that you just couldn't help brightening any room you entered?

God's favor goes with you as you trust in Him. It may not be as obvious as a big, mean bouncer. But His favor will grace your surroundings with a lot more positive results.

For it is You who blesses the righteous man,
O LORD, You surround him with favor
as with a shield.

PSALM 5:12

She leans toward the curtain on trembling legs, grasping its edge with a sweaty palm. Why in the world did I say yes to this, she thinks. So many people. All eyes on me. This is not my thing! But when the pastor had asked her to share her testimony about being set free from drug abuse, she had known it was important. Others needed to know the power of God to overcome.

Lord, I can't do this. But You can! And since You're in me, I can too. Use my heart and my body and my voice today, but use Your words. Let others see Your power as I have. Thank You!

When it's His plan and you're willing, you simply cannot fail.

I can do all things through Him
who strengthens me.
PHILIPPIANS 4:13

There is a sandwich that appears at a certain fast food chain once a year or so. When it does, it causes a frenzy. Advertising announces, It's back! And people go out of their way to spend money on this sandwich whose meat is machine-formed to look like the real thing. Meanwhile, their pantries and grocery stores are stocked with nutrient-rich fresh foods. But they flock anyway, hoping to be satisfied.

There's nothing wrong with enjoying a treat now and then. But living off of fast food would not benefit our bodies. And living off of anything but God alone would not benefit our souls. We need the real food of God to stay spiritually strong.

Why do you spend money for what is not bread, and your wages for what does not satisfy? Listen carefully to Me, and eat what is good, and delight yourself in abundance. Incline your ear and come to Me. Listen, that you may live.

ISAIAH 55:2-3

The kingdom of God is a petri dish for faith. It's got just the right Holy Spirit ingredients to grow His good works. What does this mean to you? It means you don't need to worry about people or circumstances that are out of your control (which is, by the way, everything). Your kindness in His name scatters seed. Your prayers ensure the right environment for growth. Just go about your business of living in His shadow, and pretty soon you'll see the fruit of His labor popping up all over the place.

The kingdom of God doesn't need help. But God does want you to help. He's given you a role to play for His glory and your good.

The kingdom of God is like a man who casts seed upon the soil; and he goes to bed at night and gets up by day, and the seed sprouts and grows—how, he himself does not know.

MARK 4:26-27

The surgeon answers his phone. "Hey Doc, just wanted to let you know. I watched a video on YouTube and performed my own do-it-yourself heart surgery last night. Good as new! So I guess I won't need you after all. Thanks anyway!"

No one in their right mind would attempt their own heart surgery, much less actually succeed at it! A heart patient needs the surgeon to perform his role with excellence. And guess what? We've all been heart patients at one time or another. We've all needed the precise and life-saving help of the holy Healer. It may take time to adjust to the new normal of salvation and freedom. But all the parts are in working order to live by the Spirit.

Moreover, I will give you a new heart
and put a new spirit within you;
and I will remove the heart of stone from
your flesh and give you a heart of flesh.

EZEKIEL 36:26

There's a reward that comes from simply hanging in there. Recipients of this reward don't earn it by running fast or being the best. Sometimes the race that gets them there is less than graceful: like a kitten slipping from a branch and clinging to the bark with two splayed and desperate paws. Hang in there long enough, and the hero fireman will come to the rescue. And you'll end up cuddled close in the arms of the One who loves you.

The "hang in there" reward comes to those who simply don't give up in life. They fall down again and again, but always get up and keep aiming toward Jesus.

Blessed is a man who perseveres under trial; for once he has been approved, he will receive the crown of life which the Lord has promised to those who love Him.

JAMES 1:12

She had just flown to Denver a month before, to take care of her sick friend. And then she received the sad news: her friend's dad had passed away. So without a blink, she turned right around and bought a plane ticket to Denver. Again. To offer nothing more than the ministry of presence.

This ministry requires no special training. It simply requires a person to...well, be present. To show up. It's the kind of love that says, "Whatever you need, I'm here for you."

God says to us, I will draw near to you (Js. 4:8). Never will I leave you (Heb. 13:5). When we show people that kind of nearness love, we're showing them the true heart of God.

Therefore I urge you, brethren, by the mercies of God, to present your bodies a living and holy sacrifice, acceptable to God, which is your spiritual service of worship.

ROMANS 12:1

The damsel is tied tight, a short distance from the locomotive barreling in her direction with whistle blaring. The cowboy leaps to the tracks with his knife—knowing that unless things change, he will most certainly die within seconds.

Our hero doesn't hesitate. He knows that his sidekick is around the bend at the depot, working to get the tracks shifted just in time for it to pull away from the distressed beauty. Sure enough, creaking rails shift left and the locomotive zooms past, coal-stained wind blowing severed ropes away from the maid and her tall-hatted companion.

Things with Jesus were way more serious. But the idea exists: Jesus jumped in before conditions were perfect. And His actions are what made the shift for us, from certain death to eternal life.

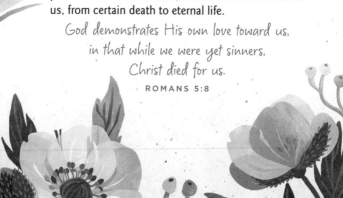

God demonstrates His own love toward us,
in that while we were yet sinners,
Christ died for us.
ROMANS 5:8

Cast: to throw, fling or send; that is to drive from, by force. To drive or impel by violence. Casting cares on the Lord can be a strong action! It can imply forcefully, deliberately not taking on worry or anxiety when tempted. Instead, when you cast your cares on Him, you say, "I'm trusting God with this! I refuse to let the enemy get under my skin!"

cast: to sow; to scatter seed. Casting cares on the Lord can also mean giving Him whatever shreds of good there are, and allowing Him to work them together for good (Rom. 8:28). Casting, in this sense, is telling God (and your own heart) that you trust Him to bring beauty from ashes.

(Definitions from Webster's 1828 Dictionary)

Cast your burden upon the LORD and He will sustain you; He will never allow the righteous to be shaken.

PSALM 55:22

A stranger comes up to the ministry team after the service. He tearfully tells Charles his worry: his son has been born many weeks prematurely and the outlook is bleak.

Charles feels a tug on his heart. "Sir, I'm so glad you came to me today. My granddaughter was born weighing just a pound and a half. Today she is a healthy six-year-old. Let's pray for the Lord to do it again."

Our experiences serve to teach and train us about God and His character. Our experiences can also minister to others who go through similar pain. Circumstances may not be exactly the same, but the character of God does not change across circumstances. He is God in the same way, every time.

Blessed be the God and Father of our Lord Jesus Christ, the Father of mercies and God of all comfort, who comforts us in all our affliction so that we will be able to comfort those who are in any affliction with the comfort with which we ourselves are comforted by God.

II CORINTHIANS 1:3-4

Cale watches Abraham the fish floating upside down at the surface of the tank. "He's going to live, Mom."

"Buddy, I just don't think so. He's pretty dead."

"Yes but Jesus can raise him. He died too soon. Abraham's going to live." Cale goes to sleep with a smile on his face.

In the morning when Mom walks in to wake Cale, she gasps. "Honey! Wake up!" Cale bounces out of bed and walks to the fish tank. "Good morning, Abraham! I knew you'd come back!"

Unswerving hope requires faith like a child. Even if we haven't seen that particular miracle in our own lives before, we can be sure God can do it. Stay strong despite the opposition!

Let us hold fast the confession
of our hope without wavering,
for He who promised is faithful.
HEBREWS 10:23

One man didn't like the way his neighbor cared for his front yard. So he built a 6-foot fence between them. It cost him a lot of money. The rest of the neighborhood thought it was an eyesore. It made others wonder if the man were friendly, and they stopped inviting him to block parties. When the man's son started dating his neighbor's daughter, he wanted to be kind. But he felt guilty about his fence. So he stayed hidden behind it.

Offenses are similar. They set up an "O"-shaped fence around a person's heart, keeping them from the fullness of joy. If you have an offense, ask Holy Spirit what it would cost to tear it down and start fresh.

So he got up and came to his father. But while he was still a long way off, his father saw him and felt compassion for him, and ran and embraced him and kissed him.

LUKE 15:20

The young woman's story was fascinating. Her picture had been sent accidentally to a young couple in the United States. The couple felt the calling, and adopted the tiny, malnourished orphan in the height of Ethiopia's famine. In her thirties, the woman went back to visit the orphanage where she had her earliest memories. She had studied to become a nutritionist, specializing in how to provide nourishment in developing countries.

Each of us has been lifted from a dark life into a royal kingdom. We have gifts, passion, and abilities based on our experiences and callings. He has hand-picked each of us, equipped us abundantly, and commissioned us to bring the light of hope!

For He rescued us from the domain of darkness, and transferred us to the kingdom of His beloved Son, in whom we have redemption, the forgiveness of sins.

COLOSSIANS 1:13-14

*Y*ou sit trembling in the cell along with several angry activists. You aren't quite sure how your shopping trip turned into this! There'd been a loud crowd on a street corner. You got caught in it. And here you are, accidentally arrested!

But your boss had been across the street in a coffee shop when it happened. He sprinted straight to the jail. "I know that woman," he said to the police commissioner, whom he knows well. "Her name is Sara. She was just a passerby." In no time you are released, and the error is erased from your files.

There is One who is always working on your behalf. You may not see what He's up to, but you can know He's in your favor.

But now, thus says the LORD, your Creator,
O Jacob, and He who formed you, O Israel,
"Do not fear, for I have redeemed you; I have
called you by name; you are Mine!"

ISAIAH 43:1

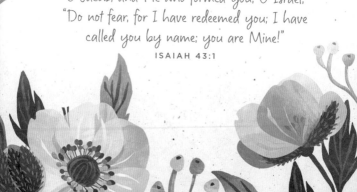

It's not your job to manage others' actions. You can't change how a person will see you and respond.

But there is One who sees you all the time. He's the one whose opinion matters. He asks you to consistently look in His direction for guidance. That way, when you're in situations that are unfamiliar or emotional, you won't need to rely on your guesses of what to do. He always knows the way through.

Integrity means acting the same when no one is looking, as you would when all eyes are on you. Make a lifestyle out of living like you're being scrutinized. Because chances are, someone is watching. And you are an example of the light of Jesus.

Keep your behavior excellent among the Gentiles, so that in the thing in which they slander you as evildoers, they may because of your good deeds, as they observe them, glorify God in the day of visitation.

I PETER 2:12

"What do you see, captain?" The intercom buzzes with static as you wait for a response. "Come on up and see!" You climb to the top deck and into the main cabin. The captain hands you his binoculars.

It's land! You see excited family members jumping up and down on shore, excited to welcome your ship home.

Corrie Ten Boom once made the observation that the underside of a needlework is full of confusing thread ends and mixed-up colors. But the top side is a beautiful picture. Right now, what we see dimly (1 Cor. 13:12), the Lord sees clearly. He invites us to come see things from His point of view. All we need to do is ask.

Therefore if you have been raised up with Christ, keep seeking the things above, where Christ is, seated at the right hand of God.

COLOSSIANS 3:1

Nothing from God is wasted. Absolutely nothing! That means that beyond our needs, which He always provides—God also supplies us with gifts, treasures, and resources to be put to good use. If He only gave you what you needed for survival, then what would you have to give away? Loving others is a necessary part of your life!

He knows what you need to sustain your life and stay healthy. He also knows that an overflow of favor, love, grace, and mercy works in everyone's favor. So He is very generous. He gives each of us way more than is necessary. So be generous right back. Who needs what you have to give away today?

He humbled you and let you be hungry, and fed you with manna which you did not know, nor did your fathers know, that He might make you understand that man does not live by bread alone, but man lives by everything that proceeds out of the mouth of the LORD.

DEUTERONOMY 8:3

In January 1945, troops barged into Auschwitz, the largest Nazi concentration camp that existed. They rescued over 6000 emaciated Jews at that time. One can only imagine the feeling at seeing strong, healthy men with guns fighting on their behalf and carrying them gently to freedom.

There will be a day when all of us experience freedom like we've never known. Every sorrow, every injustice, every hurt will be swallowed up by the victory of Jesus. Suffering will disappear. Disease will be forgotten. Your worst wounds will be gently, lovingly treated. Faith will be a thing of the past, because we will know. Only love will remain.

For the Lord Himself will descend from heaven with a shout, with the voice of the archangel and with the trumpet of God, and the dead in Christ will rise first.

I THESSALONIANS 4:16

A tree, in simply being its tree-ness, is a most glorious sight. It follows the Law of God to a tee. The night sky, in its twinkly beauty or cloud-covered darkness, is glorious. It never questions who or what it is; who or what God is. It knows.

Being still and quiet in nature is a powerful way to see God at work. Insects crawling, brooks gurgling, and breezes dancing through grass all reflect the sovereignty of God.

Step away from distraction today if you can. Find a quiet place outside. And drink in His power through the simplest, subtlest beauty of nature.

The heavens are telling of the glory of God;
and their expanse is declaring the work
of His hands. Day to day pours forth speech,
and night to night reveals knowledge.

PSALM 19:1-2

According to Webster's 1828 Dictionary, *expectation* is the prospect of good to come.

The definition of expectation does not specify what sort of good is to come. There is a way to expect certain things to happen; and if they don't that leads to disappointment.

But if you learn to place your expectation in God alone—believing that He is good, and that He will do good—you will not be disappointed. You will notice Him showing up in ways that surprise you.

Like a child leaping down the stairs on Christmas morning, expectancy is full of all sorts of hope. Take the challenge today to bound into the day with a hopeful prayer of very good things to come.

In the morning, O LORD, You will hear my voice; in the morning I will order my prayer to You and eagerly watch.

PSALM 5:3

There was nothing they could do. The final decision for Gabriel's adoption lay with the board of a foreign country. There was no information line to call; no friend in the system who could track down answers. All they could do was wait.

But they were confident of this: that God had brought Gabriel to them. They knew they had done everything they could to process things correctly and show their interest in adopting this child. And they knew that where their ability ended, God's had only begun.

God only asks us to do what we can. He will do what we can't.

Wait for the LORD; be strong and let your heart take courage; yes, wait for the LORD.
PSALM 27:14

Parenting is arguably the hardest and most rewarding profession in the world. Where else does a person care that much, love that hard, and have the least amount of control over the final results? There may be glimpses of the reward at times. But mostly, a parent gets up the morning determined to do their best—and goes to bed at night praying for God's love to cover over mistakes and cultivate seeds.

It may not come until years later, when a child is grown—or maybe not ever, this side of heaven. But parenting yields wonderful kingdom results. A parent who invests in their child by investing in God's lead, blesses His heart.

Let us not lose heart in doing good, for in due time we will reap if we do not grow weary.

GALATIANS 6:9

The body of Christ is supposed to look different than the rest of the world. We should love the hardest, show the most grace for one another, excel in conflict resolution, forgive the soonest, and work well together.

Of course, the devil despises unity. So he works against it. Loving our fellow believers well can be harder than loving strangers. When one of our own hurts us, the offenses and pain can run deep.

But God is in this. He is working in us and among us. He is on our side. Our weapons of grace and forgiveness can cut the devil to the heart, every time. So use them often!

So then, while we have opportunity,
let us do good to all people, and especially
to those who are of the household of the faith.

GALATIANS 6:10

"It's a thankless house I live in," she grumbles. Four boys and a husband. Messy, stinky, hungry, and loud. Thank you is not a phrase that passes the lips of this crew unless she prompts them with "What do you say?" This is her life?

But in the quiet of night, when the boys are in bed and she wipes down countertops, God speaks softly in her heart. He soothes her aching spirit and reminds her of all the good things that wouldn't have happened today if there were no boys to do things for, no husband to partner with.

Just then, the sleepy-eyed youngest wanders downstairs. "Night Mama. Love you." And in that moment, everything is full of thanks indeed.

With good will render service, as to the Lord, and not to men, knowing that whatever good thing each one does, this he will receive back from the Lord, whether slave or free.

EPHESIANS 6:7-8

The dance instructor stands in front of her eager girls. "This routine is a good one! You're going to love it!" The girls know from experience that hours and hours of work will be put in. Muscles will ache. Toes will get cramped. Tumbles may happen. But in the end, the joy of dancing together makes every inch of effort pay off.

We may not know exactly what's coming, but we can trust it's going to be good. We have experience with the goodness of God: either personally, through His Word, or through the stories of others. Trust the plan Maker, and every inch of effort will pay off.

"For I know the plans that I have for you," declares the LORD, "plans for welfare and not for calamity to give you a future and a hope."

JEREMIAH 29:11

The very first song in the Bible was sung in victory. Egypt had been chasing Israel through the desert, when the escaped slaves came toe to toe with the Red Sea. At the Lord's command, Moses parted the waters and a million Israelites passed through on dry land. And then the Egyptian soldiers, with their fast horses and sharp swords, were swallowed by the crashing waves of the sea returning to rest.

Moses' sister couldn't contain herself! The miracle was too amazing; the victory was too...well, victorious! And so she sang. And others joined in. What had appeared to be imminent death for them all, became God's great defeat. Because, man in his power, is hardly the tiniest fraction of God in His.

Some boast in chariots and some in horses,
but we will boast in the name of the LORD,
our God.

PSALM 20:7

If you ask someone what skydiving is like, they might say exhilarating, or terrifying, or like jumping out of a flying airplane! But until you strap yourself into that harness...until you listen to the training, sign a waiver saying you know you could die, take off, wait for the count, and then push off the edge into ear-splitting winds as you plummet to the earth...you can't ever really know what skydiving is like.

God's answers often come through experience. Because by knowing instead of just hearing, we get all the feelings and understanding that can come no other way. God's character is revealed in experience. And we gain compassion for others when we've been there ourselves.

Call to Me and I will answer you, and I will tell you great and mighty things, which you do not know.

JEREMIAH 33:3

During both world wars, carrier pigeons were a stealthy and powerful way to communicate. They could fly high and fast, and had the ability to find home again. They were often decorated as war heroes for successfully completing many messaging missions between soldiers behind the lines.

God's Word is even more reliable than a homing pigeon. What He sends out always serves its purpose. It never returns empty-handed. When you lovingly speak truth to someone, whether they receive it or not, it plants seeds. When you encourage a neighbor, love is spread in a most necessary way. When you read the Bible, whether you think it has stuck in your mind or not, your soul benefits no matter what.

So will My word be which goes forth from My mouth; it will not return to Me empty, without accomplishing what I desire, And without succeeding in the matter for which I sent it.

ISAIAH 55:11

How could anyone doubt God? How could anyone miss the most unspeakable generosity of love and grace? If you've truly experienced Him on a personal level, you know you can never go back.

See if you can think of a time, one or two or ten years ago, when you were burdened heavily with a relationship or sin. One that made you feel helpless and horrible. Compare that situation to now. Is it different? Better? Gone? If you live life in the Spirit, chances are your current situation looks absolutely nothing like the past. And if the situation itself still looks the same, you are most certainly being changed on the inside.

He saved us, not on the basis of deeds which we have done in righteousness, but according to His mercy, by the washing of regeneration and renewing by the Holy Spirit, whom He poured out upon us richly through Jesus Christ our Savior.

TITUS 3:5-6

He had always secretly hoped his son would take on the family furniture business. But Alan had a passion for structural engineering. And he was on the phone now, announcing that he had an entry level position at a large firm in Chicago. "Alan I am so proud of you! You've worked so hard in school, and the way I've seen you networking lately has truly impressed me. The engineering world is better for having you! Never mind the furniture business...the Lord has plans for that too! I'm sure He'll reveal them in time. Go, son! Use your gifts!

Our Father is our biggest cheerleader. What the world thinks is far inferior to the tune of the Lord's delight in our ears and hearts.

Let them shout for joy and rejoice, who favor my vindication; and let them say continually, "The LORD be magnified, who delights in the prosperity of His servant."

PSALM 35:27

Can you imagine how magnificent our heavenly Father is? So magnificent that for those whose role is to worship Him on His throne, they never tire of declaring what they see: Holy, holy, holy is the Lord God Almighty! Imagine that every time they blink, those creatures see a new radiance emanating from Him. Imagine that His color and shape and light are constantly shifting into more beauty.

Think of the most awe-striking thing you've ever seen. Your baby's birth...the top of a mountain or depth of a canyon...and then multiply that by infinity. Who and what God is will keep us casting our crowns and falling on our faces in utter joy for the rest of our eternal lives.

Then I looked, and I heard the voice of many angels around the throne and the living creatures and the elders; and the number of them was myriads of myriads, and thousands of thousands.

REVELATION 5:11-12

The stock market had been shaky for several days. She was hesitant to move her investments. But she was scared to leave them as is. She couldn't sleep. She barely ate. The anxiety was making her hair fall out, she thought, as she stepped out of the shower. If the market crashed, she would be crushed. She'd lose her house, her car, her dog, her lifestyle...

Nothing on earth deserves that kind of reverence. God knows the world is too unstable for us to trust in anything or anyone but Him. He wants our whole heart, because He is the only One who can shelter it well. Surrender everything to God, and His peace will take the place of terror every time.

> For where your treasure is,
> there your heart will be also.
> LUKE 12:34

God made people, and people have made gods. His nonstop love has given us free will. Free will has allowed us to leave Him and search for other things.

Any gods created by people are just...wood. Or metal. Or figments of imagination. But nothing—no one—can hold a candle to the King of Kings.

The kingdom of darkness has no creative ideas. They may act on convenience, using people's desire to worship as an opportunity to manipulate them into worshiping wood or metal. But there is only One to worship.

Check your heart today—do you worship the one true God with all of your heart, soul, mind and strength? Or have you divided your gods?

Thus says the LORD, the King of Israel and his Redeemer, the LORD of hosts: "I am the first and I am the last, and there is no God besides Me.... Do not tremble and do not be afraid; have I not long since announced it to you and declared it? And you are My witnesses. Is there any God besides Me, or is there any other Rock? I know of none."

ISAIAH 44:6, 8

Many years ago, it was common for people to own a family Bible. The front of the Bible often contained a family tree, listing ancestors' birth and death and marriage dates. Family Bibles were and are a treasure!

And many families own the personal Bibles of faithful grandparents or great-grandparents. The ones who went before, who set a foundation of faith for their family's name.

Legacy is valuable in the kingdom of heaven. Any person who sets the tone for the ones coming after them, is setting their family up for great blessing. So thank the Lord for all in your family who have gone before in faith. And set your heart to be that for your family members to come.

The memory of the righteous is blessed.
PROVERBS 10:7

Of all the Christmas, birthday, and just-because gifts a person receives, the Holy Spirit is the best. Jesus sent the Spirit of God as a gift of Presence. His presence is comfort, guidance, wisdom, and a deposit for the infinite treasures of heaven.

We don't have to earn Him. Our bodies and spirits don't have to look a certain way or be a certain amount of clean for Him to come in and make His home. In fact, He's a very good housecleaner. He'll get the job done.

All the Holy Spirit asks is for you to receive Him. Welcome Him in, and you'll never be without the greatest gift known to man for the rest of your life.

I am with you always,
even to the end of the age.

MATTHEW 28:20

Grandparents are crafted with a built-in desire to lavish love. Generosity oozes from their pores. Lipstick covers the faces of those whose grandmothers have bright pink lips.

And so, several years ago smart banks began offering college funds. These funds allow grandparents (or others) to invest a very small amount at the time their grandbaby is born. Over eighteen years, the fund grows to the point of being enough for further education if the child chooses. At that point, the money is available to the adult grandchild.

God's inheritance is even grander, although it matures along with us as we receive Him and follow His lead. When the time is right, each of us is welcomed with the lavishing kisses of His glorious inheritance in heaven.

Then the King will say to those on His right, "Come, you who are blessed of My Father, inherit the kingdom prepared for you from the foundation of the world."

MATTHEW 25:34

The young scout was struggling under the weight of his pack. He had fallen behind the troop, exhausted from the hike and they were barely halfway to camp! But troop leader Jim sat on a rock ahead. "Hey buddy! Why is your pack such a burden?" The scout removed his pack and opened the top. Several large rocks—new ones for his collection—spilled out. "Hmm. I love your hobby. Maybe I can carry those for you for now?" Instantly the scout's pack felt about 20 pounds lighter (which it was!).

Jesus doesn't want us to carry anything that could harm us or weigh us down. But He Himself can handle everything that concerns us! What are you carrying today that would be much easier for Him?

Therefore humble yourselves under the mighty hand of God, that He may exalt you at the proper time, casting all your anxiety on Him, because He cares for you.

1 PETER 5:6-7

The coffee pot broke on the morning of your big parent-teacher conference day. You won't have time to stop at a drive-through. But you can stay awake and alert...because Jesus.

The doctor hands you a booklet on how to handle your new diagnosis, with prospects of maintaining it but probably never being cured. But you have hope...because Jesus.

She wants a divorce. You know she's not thinking straight, and you know she knows divorce isn't the answer. You feel hopeless and panicked. But know there is a way through...because Jesus.

Nothing is too little for Him. Nothing is too big for Him. Because all of the things pertain to you...and you, my friend, are His favorite.

These things I have spoken to you, so that in Me you may have peace. In the world you have tribulation, but take courage; I have overcome the world.

JOHN 16:33

The dog shivered in the back yard cage. She was scared, emaciated, and weather-worn. The rescuers gathered her and transported her to safety. They named her Joy.

Daily, Dr. Villa stepped inside Joy's cage with a bowl of food. He sat at the far end and waited. Joy stayed in her corner at first. Little by little, she began inching forward on paws and elbows—one day to sniff the food, one day to eat it, and one day to crawl past the empty bowl toward the doctor. It wasn't until Joy's nose touched Dr. Villa's knee one day that he touched her back. And that was the beginning of Joy's true rehabilitation into love.

God waits until we're ready. But when we move, He moves.

Draw near to God and
He will draw near to you.

JAMES 4:8

Is our love supply bottomless or boxed in? Imagine a woman examining her cupboard when her neighbor asks for a cup of sugar. "I have about two cups left. I might want it later, so I can give you just a tablespoon now." The neighbor will remember this moment. And if the woman needs two eggs for a recipe later, the neighbor may respond, "I have four eggs and I may be extra hungry tomorrow morning. So I can give you just one egg now."

Our heart status matters more than our pocket status. Are we acting out of love, or with respect to what we think we can spare? Whatever our hearts pour out is how much room we have to receive.

Give, and it will be given to you. They will pour into your lap a good measure—pressed down, shaken together, and running over. For by your standard of measure it will be measured to you in return.

LUKE 6:38

What mountain are you facing today?

It may look like a project whose parameters are truly impossible. It may be a broken relationship with a parent or child—one that you've tried and failed to fix in the past. It may be depression or disease or discouragement.

Don't give up. Do not give up! The devil wants every believer to crumble under the weight of "What if" and "I can't."

Well the devil is right. You are right! You can't! But that's not a weakness, it's a strength! Your weakness is what invites God to give you His might. You can't. But He can. All it takes is faith, patience, and connection to His heart.

And He said to them, "Because of the littleness of your faith; for truly I say to you, if you have faith the size of a mustard seed, you will say to this mountain, 'Move from here to there,' and it will move; and nothing will be impossible to you."

MATTHEW 17:20

God knows our weaknesses. And acknowledging them before God gives Him room to wield His strength. But there's a way to do that doubtfully, and a way to do it with faith.

If you're using your weakness as an argument for why not, then you're not operating in faith. A lack of faith can actually block God from fully working on your behalf!

But if you're confessing your weakness to express your need to Him, then there's no limit to what He can do. Just check your heart and make sure your posture before God is open to possibilities. Most likely, His plan for success won't look much like what you think it should.

The LORD said to him (Moses), "Who has made man's mouth? Or who makes him mute or deaf, or seeing or blind? Is it not I, the LORD? Now then go, and I, even I, will be with your mouth, and teach you what you are to say."

EXODUS 4:11-12

No one could ever accuse Jesus of being politically correct! He was true to His heart, which was true to His Father.

"If you eat my flesh and drink my blood...." Possibly the most head-turning sermon ever. And it scared away many.

"Oh, you don't want to follow Me quite yet? If you turn back to the plough now your heart is divided. No man who turns back can follow Me."

"My mom and brothers are here to see Me? So? My real mom and brothers are those who believe in Me."

When confronted with Jesus, a person will either be drawn in or pushed away. God is divisive—and that's what makes Him trustworthy, unchanging, and true.

For the word of God is living and active and sharper than any two-edged sword, and piercing as far as the division of soul and spirit, of both joints and marrow, and able to judge the thoughts and intentions of the heart.

HEBREWS 4:12

Some people feel pretty good about the course of this nation, and some do not. Perhaps the course of the nation depends less on our leaders, though—and more on the intercession of the Saints?

Pharaoh was a man who believed he was a god. But the Lord used him for the good of His chosen people.

Nebuchadnezzar (Dan. 4:28-37) was king of a pagan nation. God gave him a warning, and then a very unusual method of rehabilitation. In the end Nebuchadnezzar praised the Lord.

It's easy to be distressed by what we see—but we can choose to be emboldened by what we don't see. The more we seek God and pray, the more we'll be in line with His plans for our future.

For the Scripture says to Pharaoh,
"FOR THIS VERY PURPOSE I RAISED YOU UP,
TO DEMONSTRATE MY POWER IN YOU,
AND THAT MY NAME MIGHT BE PROCLAIMED
THROUGHOUT THE WHOLE EARTH."

ROMANS 9:17

"One day about thirty years ago, my neighbor told me I was a bad mom," a friend shared over coffee. "Those words have stayed with me through the raising of my children. Only last week, this woman and I had a moment of reconciliation."

Words stick. They bring life, or they tear down. Words are powerful—because God is the all-powerful Word.

We have the amazing power to say something that will bring out another person's greatest strengths and confidence. We can also say something that will dishearten another person and do long-lasting damage.

That kind of power only belongs in one place: in the hands of the Holy Spirit, who can help guide and guard our lips.

Set a guard, O LORD, over my mouth;
keep watch over the door of my lips.

PSALM 141:3

The student stares, dumbfounded, at her professor's remarks. The class: Organic chemistry lab. The grade: D. Why? Not because of her formulas or attendance. I told all students at the beginning of the semester to wear goggles in the lab. On October 12 your goggles were around your neck and not your eyes. Almost-failure. Because one day she forgot the rules.

God is quick to forgive. Slow to anger. He gives warnings and tips. He provides direction, both written and as He speaks on a daily basis. He's not into religion. He has laws in place, but He is intent on our success. So life with the Lord is an open Book test.

The LORD is compassionate and gracious, slow
to anger and abounding in lovingkindness...
He has not dealt with us according to our sins,
nor rewarded us according to our iniquities.

PSALM 103:8, 10

Some gifts happen because of obligation, like at your boss's boss's Christmas party gift exchange. Other gifts are given out of love. The very best gifts are often ones which demonstrate that the giver knows the recipient, and has given much thought to the recipient's likes.

God's gifts are sometimes tangible. Sometimes given from His hand to yours, through another person. And sometimes His gifts are intangible, like grace when you need it most or an answer you've been waiting for faithfully.

Every gift from God shows how well He knows us. Individually and lovingly. He thinks about us all the time. He chooses His gifts according to what He knows will bless our hearts.

Every good thing given and every perfect gift is from above, coming down from the Father of lights, with whom there is no variation or shifting shadow.

JAMES 1:17

"Yeah, I did a marathon course once. In my car." But to the man who trains for nine months, gets up early, shivers at the starting line, and listens to his own feet hit the pavement for twenty-six point two miles before crossing Finish, that medal around his neck represents much more than going from point A to point B. It means not giving up. Replacing doubt with knowing. He has gained the knowledge that he can indeed do way more than he ever thought possible. The man who drives the marathon route has no such experience under his belt.

There's no shortcut to maturity in Christ. Persevering with God comes with its own kind of unique reward—and it is so worth the work.

And let endurance have its perfect result,
so that you may be perfect and complete,
lacking in nothing.

JAMES 1:4

Church is not a building. Church is a lifestyle. It is every man, woman, and child who loves Jesus. Many people have become disillusioned by the organization we've called church—man-made processes and programs meant to make the Church get along well.

Staying away from groups in buildings, because of those buildings' organizations, is like never eating healthy foods because you don't like to wait in line at the grocery store. Your own body will suffer for it.

We were made for community. You need it, and we need you. Yes, people make life more complicated. But it's the simplest thing in the world to love Jesus among others who are loving Him too.

Let us consider how to stimulate one another to love and good deeds, not forsaking our own assembling together, as is the habit of some, but encouraging one another; and all the more as you see the day drawing near.

HEBREWS 10:24-25

Think of someone you know who is wise. How would you describe them? Would you say they're full of anxiety and foolish words? Or would you more likely say they're a calming and gracious presence?

Wisdom birthed from experience is like a holy sedative. Wisdom calms the spirit and relaxes the soul. When one knows because they've been there, not a single person or fear can steal that joy away.

Not much can shake the wisest of people, because they've been shaken before and still remain standing. Stronger than ever, and more sure of their Foundation. Be thankful for the wise examples in your life today.

A man's discretion makes him slow to anger, and it is his glory to overlook a transgression.

PROVERBS 19:11

She wrestled with the same relationship conflict for seven years. Countless times, she was on her face in her closet. "I can't do this God! What do I do! You've got to come through and help!" Every day it went inch forward...or a half inch back. Her desperation never left. But neither did He. It was a training exercise called How to Cling to the Rock.

And in the end when, after seven years the relationship began healing, she was scrappier. Stronger. Wiser. Less prone to silly choices, and more sure of His presence in any storm.

God is our refuge and strength,
a very present help in trouble.

PSALM 46:1

Some see God's warnings as harsh and demanding. But consider His cautions as extremely helpful information.

God does not vengefully say, "If you trust in people instead of Me, I'm going to curse you, you rotten traitor!" He says, "Be careful because I want you to know this. If you trust in people, it will lead to brokenness."

Likewise, God does not bribe us by saying, "If you choose Me, I'll give you all kinds of sweets!" Instead, He says, "Listen carefully, because I want you to know this. If you trust Me, you'll feel a major difference. You'll learn over time what a true Partner and Friend I am to those who love Me."

Thus says the LORD, "Cursed is the man who trusts in mankind and makes flesh his strength, and whose heart turns away from the LORD.... Blessed is the man who trusts in the LORD and whose trust is the LORD."

JEREMIAH 17:5, 7

Imagine a day when there will be no more confusion. No more cultures and nations who choose their own gods and live by their own code of truth. There will be a day when our God will take His place before the whole earth, and rule in all His glorious majesty. The devil will fall once and for all.

We get to look forward to that. Others, whether they realize it or not, are living under the influence of the devil's fear of that day. They need the truth revealed to them!

The kingdom of heaven is big enough for anyone who believes. Who in your life needs freedom from a life of fear?

And I heard a loud voice from the throne, saying, "Behold, the tabernacle of God is among men, and He will dwell among them, and they shall be His people, and God Himself will be among them."

REVELATION 21:3

"Ugh, I'm so ugly and ridiculous."

"Willa, let me ask you something. Do you think I have bad taste?"

"No, of course not!"

"You think I have good taste?"

"Actually really good, yes!"

"Okay then. I like you. I think you're beautiful. And I have good taste. So I guess you have to believe me!"

God has the very best taste, and He does literally nothing on accident. The mere fact of your existence—all of your glorious cells and fibers and flesh—is a walking miracle. You'll always be able to point out flaws if you look for them. It's best to choose to believe: You are a masterpiece.

I will give thanks to You, for I am fearfully and wonderfully made; wonderful are Your works, and my soul knows it very well.

PSALM 139:14

Good: valid; not weak or defective; not false; complete or sufficiently perfect in its kind.

What is your definition of good? Maybe at the dentist's office, good means no cavities. Maybe at the grocery store, good means a sale on steak. Maybe in a perfect world, good means someone giving you a Ferrari!

If you have a hard time believing today's Scripture that every good thing is at your fingertips—maybe it's not that the statement is untrue. Maybe it's your definition of good that needs an adjustment.

The next time you feel deprived of something, ask the Lord if what you want is good in His eyes. Then allow Him to lead you to the good things He's stored up for you today!

They who seek the LORD shall not be in want of any good thing.

PSALM 34:10

Tattoos have become much more mainstream. Jesus has always said, Come as you are; I can work with it! But more commonly than ever, believers, too, are ending up inked. Same with piercings and the occasional craft beer. What are we to think of this? Is it unbiblical? Does it offend God? Should it offend us?

It's easy to see what's seeable, and that's where a person's mind dwells. But the mind of God searches the heart of mankind—in places no human can see. A person gives off truer signals about their spiritual needs than just the visible. Watch behaviors and words more than pierced eyebrows or inked arms—and you may begin to spot the needs worth going after.

But the LORD said to Samuel, "Do not look at his appearance or at the height of his stature, because I have rejected him; for God sees not as man sees, for man looks at the outward appearance, but the LORD looks at the heart."

1 SAMUEL 16:7

In the beginning, God created. It began with a desire, then an idea, then a demand: "Let there be light." And there was.

What makes us stumble at the thought of God being able to create new from nothing? When we walk on an earth that pulses with His heartbeat for us. When our own heartbeats match the rhythm of His love.

It's somehow easier to imagine His creative miracles of long ago. Not so easy to believe He will straighten that scoliosis or make just the right job materialize for your skill set.

When in doubt, trap that doubt with a legion of truths: God is Creator. He created, He creates, and He will create—even today, even right now.

In the beginning God created the heavens and the earth.

GENESIS 1:1

Pots of chili lined the cafeteria countertop, along with bowls of every delicious and cheesy topping known to man. There were rolls and cornbread, and a smorgasbord of desserts enough to topple any sugar-sensitive someone.

Two hundred employees placed the suggested donation and then some in a jar. For every dollar given, the company had agreed to match the contribution.

For a warehouse worker and his wife, the cancer diagnosis of their baby seemed just a tad bit less lonely and scary. Watching their fellow employees pour out love as they dished out chili was a spirit strengthener for sure.

As a servant in God's house you can believe—you will be taken care of.

You whom I have taken from the ends of the earth, and called from its remotest parts and said to you, "You are My servant, I have chosen you and not rejected you."

ISAIAH 41:9-10

A pauper lives like the next meal is unsure. He stores away his money, unable to share and afraid to spend. His friendships are guarded and distant: What if they needed or asked something of me? I can't afford to give! He needs more than he gives.

A prince (or princess), lives like the next meal will surely satisfy him. He invests his money wisely and makes giving a part of his budget. His friendships are open and fruitful: Am I the very best, most welcoming person I can be? I can't wait to give today! He serves more than he expects.

God is the God of abundance. Do you doubt that (pauper) or believe it (prince)?

Jude, a bond-servant of Jesus Christ, and brother of James, to those who are the called, beloved in God the Father, and kept for Jesus Christ: may mercy and peace and love be multiplied to you.

JUDE 1-2

Tonight, we know. We sense the presence of the King. Tonight is the time to set aside the hustle and bustle. To release the "undones" and welcome the moments of peace and reflection and joy.

Tonight, the earth holds its breath in expectation. The Father leans in. He cradles the mothers, the birthing, the desperate, the homeless—Just wait, He whispers. In just the right moment, He exhales...and the tiniest breath of hope arises from the humblest places in our hearts.

Tonight is the seed. The smallest, most power-packed yes to God's plans. The roar of the world hushes silent, because we know...it is truly a holy night.

Looking for the blessed hope
and the appearing of the glory of
our great God and Savior, Christ Jesus.

TITUS 2:13

"Where are you headed," the train conductor asks. Um...not sure? "Well this is the place to be. Get on here, the end of the line, and follow it all the way to the most beautiful place in the country. Come on! I'm sure you could use the company, and I could use a friend! I'll even pay for your ticket."

Jesus is always the beginning of the journey, whether you've known Him forever or not at all. He's the path to perfection. The door to deliverance. The hallway of hope. Anyone who takes His outreached hand is walking in the very best way.

It begins here. Right now. A fresh start and a new beginning of all things good.

For God so loved the world, that He gave
His only begotten Son, that whoever believes
in Him shall not perish, but have eternal life.
JOHN 3:16

God is the beginning of everything. He's doing a new thing in you right now! And He's capable of doing a new thing in your situation.

God is also the final say in everything. A wise pastor says, "I've read the end of the Book and it turns out great. If your situation right now isn't great, then it's definitely not the end!"

In the family of God, there is literally nothing to fear. Hold onto hope, and you'll shine with it. Let go of hope and you'll fizzle out.

Rejoice again today that Jesus is. There's no gift greater than that.

"I am the Alpha and the Omega,"
says the Lord God, "who is and who was
and who is to come, the Almighty."

REVELATION 1:8

"Who are you texting now? You've been on your phone all day!"

She rolls her eyes with a smile. "It's my dad. He's constantly checking on me. All he sends is emojis. Just dumb little reminders that he loves me."

And then the day came when she was in a car accident, and her dad was the first one she called.

Because like an attentive dad, our Father is right there. All the time. Sending little reminders of His love. Some people call them His "kisses." And when we need Him most, calling on our Father is easier than hitting Send. Because He's right there, waiting with baited breath, to remember His love.

For what great nation is there
that has a god so near to it as is the LORD
our God whenever we call on Him?

DEUTERONOMY 4:7

Each day is a chance step out in boldness. That doesn't mean pride or false courage. It takes a very humble heart and a very keen awareness of our less-than abilities apart from Christ. But every day, there's a bucket of new mercies ready to shower down on you. There's a shiny suit of armor waiting to wrap you in readiness. Whatever happened yesterday—and whatever will happen tomorrow—have no part in who you choose to be today. In Whose you choose to remember you are.

You belong to the Lord. No self-consciousness or timidity will change that. The very best vessels for His kingdom are those who say, "OK, God...let's go after it! Use me however You want."

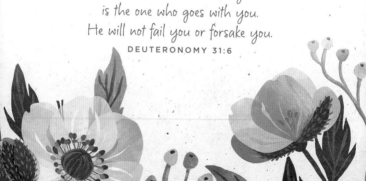

Be strong and courageous, do not be afraid or tremble at them, for the LORD your God is the one who goes with you. He will not fail you or forsake you.

DEUTERONOMY 31:6

Wherever you are today in your relationship with God, take one step further.

If you are sitting—A spectator, a waiter, a cautious not-so-sure believer—try standing.

If you are standing—An interested party, a wondering hedger, a thinker—try walking.

If you are walking—A slow mover, a curious-enough-to-act-er, a trier outer—you are ready to run.

Passionate people may stumble a bit and learn as they go. But going after God will never, ever disappoint. Keep believing that God is even bigger and better than you can possibly believe, and life with the Spirit will be a constant adventure race.

How blessed is the man who does not walk in the counsel of the wicked, nor stand in the path of sinners, nor sit in the seat of scoffers!

But his delight is in the law of the LORD, and in His law he meditates day and night.

PSALM 1:1-2

In her mid-fifties, she decided to try piano one more time. What could it hurt? She was terrible as a child—couldn't reach the keys, couldn't remember the notes, never practiced, and never got beyond book two. She had tried. But even her teacher had said she was better suited for softball.

But this time, her fingers were longer. She set aside time every day after work. And note by plunky note, her family started recognizing tunes coming from the old upright in the dining room.

God takes what was and transforms it into new beauty. Like a butterfly whose DNA still looks like the caterpillar's, the creature itself has been totally reborn. You are a new creation.

Therefore if anyone is in Christ,
he is a new creature; the old things passed
away; behold, new things have come.
II CORINTHIANS 5:17

Many people begin resolving all sorts of things about life at the end of a year. Statistically, most resolutions barely make it out of January before they crash and burn.

Instead, maybe it would be best to ask God about His resolve. What are you up to, Lord? What work are you doing in me and in the world?

Some people ask God for a single word or phrase as a theme for the upcoming year. If you ask for one and receive it, pay attention. He will lean in as you walk it out in faithfulness.

This coming year is going to be a good one...as a child of God, you can resolve to believe it!

Thus says the LORD, "Stand by the ways and see and ask for the ancient paths, where the good way is, and walk in it; and you will find rest for your souls."

JEREMIAH 6:16

LIVE YOUR FAITH

Dear Friend,

This book was prayerfully crafted with you, the reader, in mind—every word, every sentence, every page—was thoughtfully written, designed, and packaged to encourage you...right where you are this very moment. At DaySpring, our vision is to see every person experience the life-changing message of God's love. So, as we worked through rough drafts, design changes, edits, and details, we prayed for you to deeply experience His unfailing love, indescribable peace, and pure joy. It is our sincere hope that through these Truth-filled pages your heart will be blessed, knowing that God cares about you—your desires and disappointments, your challenges and dreams.

He knows. He cares. He loves you unconditionally.

BLESSINGS!
THE DAYSPRING BOOK TEAM
